SECESSIONISTS
AND OTHER
SCOUNDRELS

SECESSIONISTS
AND OTHER
SCOUNDRELS

✝

Selections from
Parson Brownlow's Book

Edited, with an Introduction, by
STEPHEN V. ASH

LOUISIANA STATE UNIVERSITY PRESS
Baton Rouge

00 02 04 06 08 07 05 03 01 99
1 3 5 4 2

Designer: Barbara Neely Bourgoyne
Typeface: Trajan; Granjon
Typesetter: Coghill Composition
Printer and binder: Edwards Brothers, Incorporated

Library of Congress Cataloging-in-Publication Data

Brownlow, William Gannaway, 1805–1877.
    [Sketches of the rise, progress, and decline of secession.
Selections]
    Secessionists and other scoundrels : selections from Parson
Brownlow's book / edited, with an introduction, by Stephen V. Ash.
        p.   cm.
    Selections from William Gannaway Brownlow's Sketches of the rise,
progress, and decline of secession.   1862.
    Includes bibliographical references and index.
    ISBN 0-8071-2353-6 (cloth : alk. paper). — ISBN 0-8071-2354-4
(pbk. : alk. paper)
    1. Secession—Southern States.   2. United States—Politics and
government—1861–1865.   3. Tennessee—Politics and
government—1861–1865.   4. Tennessee, East—History—Civil War,
1861–1865.   5. Brownlow, William Gannaway, 1805–1877.   6. Refugees—
Southern States.   I. Ash, Stephen V.   II. Title.
E458.2.B90   1999
973.7'13—dc21   98-50888
                                                                  CIP

William Gannaway Brownlow's *Sketches of the Rise, Progress, and Decline
of Secession; with a Narrative of Personal Adventures Among the Rebels*
was published in Philadelphia, 1862, by George W. Childs.
Illustrations in this edition are taken from the original.

CONTENTS

†

ILLUSTRATIONS

✝

SECESSIONISTS
AND OTHER
SCOUNDRELS

EDITOR'S INTRODUCTION

✝

In the spring of 1862, as the Civil War entered its second year, an East Tennessee newspaper editor sat down in a room of a house in New Jersey where he was temporarily residing and began assembling a book. "Assembling" describes his labors better than "writing" because most of the volume had in fact already been written, and much of it had been published—in one form or another—over the preceding years. The book was a rush job, as the author more or less admitted, but it immediately became a best seller.

The author was William Gannaway Brownlow of Knoxville, who was not only a journalist but also a Methodist preacher generally known as Parson Brownlow. The book, issued in the summer of 1862 by a Philadelphia press, was *Sketches of the Rise, Progress, and Decline of Secession; with a Narrative of Personal Adventures Among the Rebels*—but almost everybody called it by the title printed on the spine: *Parson Brownlow's Book*.

The Parson was no stranger to the public that eagerly bought and read his hastily produced volume. He had made a name for himself before the war through his newspaper, the Knoxville *Whig*, which boasted a wide readership outside as well as within Tennessee. Moreover, in the weeks before he put his book together he had conducted a very successful speaking tour of the northern states. By the time his volume hit the bookstores he was already a national celebrity.

Today, however, Brownlow has been mostly forgotten outside his home state—forgotten even by many Civil War enthusiasts. This is a shame, for he was not only an important figure in his time but also a colorful and controversial one whose editorial and oratorical diatribes are as entertaining now as they were a-hundred-and-thirty-odd years ago. Modern readers should be introduced to the Parson: that belief has inspired this volume of selections from *Parson Brownlow's Book.*

Brownlow gives us a short autobiography in the first pages of his book (see Part I within) so little need be said here about his life. Born in southwestern Virginia in 1805, he was orphaned at age eleven and placed with relatives. In 1825, at a camp meeting, he was converted; he subsequently became a Methodist circuit rider and traveled all over southern Appalachia. Eventually he settled in East Tennessee and in 1839 began publishing a newspaper—first in Elizabethton, then in Jonesboro, and finally (in 1849) in Knoxville, which he made his permanent home. In his sermons and his newspaper, as well as in numerous books, articles, pamphlets, and speeches, Brownlow promoted his pet causes. These included Methodism (the one true faith, according to the Parson), Whiggery (Henry Clay was his idol), temperance (Brownlow was a strict teetotaler), slavery (ordained by God and good for blacks as well as whites, he claimed), and the federal Union.[1] Brownlow had many enemies—at least as he saw it—and devoted most of his effort to skewering them rhetorically. The list of those castigated (some would say libeled and slandered) by the embattled Parson is a long one. It includes Baptists, Presbyterians, Catholics, Mormons, Democrats, Republicans, blacks, Irish immigrants, drinkers, Sabbath-breakers, bad poets, philandering husbands, rival editors, abolitionists, and above all, secessionists.

What Brownlow's audiences read and heard were for the most part intensely partisan harangues barbed with clever, often malicious, insults. The Parson was a skilled debater, well informed on the issues of his day and capable of arguing them on their merits, but his real forte was the ad hominem attack; he was a master of it. His prose and oratory were devoid of the polished phrasing, elegant circumlocution, and classical allusions that many prominent figures of his era employed, for Brownlow was a plainspoken man, a self-educated product of the frontier. But what he lacked in refinement he made up for in scathing wit.

1. Readers interested in knowing more about Brownlow's life can consult the sources listed in the Selected Bibliography.

Of abolitionist Harriet Beecher Stowe, author of *Uncle Tom's Cabin,* he proclaimed, "She is as ugly as Original sin—an abomination in the eyes of civilized people. A tall, course [*sic*], vulgar-looking woman— stoop-shouldered with a long yellow neck, and a long peaked nose— through which she speaks."

He likewise skewered Andrew Johnson, Democratic governor of Tennessee, in a speech delivered on the public square in Nashville: "I . . . pronounce your Governor, here upon his own dunghill, an UN-MITIGATED LIAR AND CALUMNIATOR, and a VILLAIN-OUS COWARD. . . . [T]here are better men than Andrew Johnson in our Penitentiary."

On Mormons, he had this to say: "If [Democratic president James] Buchanan would send an army to Utah, and exterminate the entire Mormon race, we will declare in favor of his administration."

On a rival newspaper, this: "[I]t has, from first to last, been edited by more *broke down Preachers,* and lewd, lying, irresponsible men, than any other single sheet in existence. And yet, in point of depravity, a want of honor, and a total disregard for truth, its present Editor is a head and shoulders taller than any ruffian who has yet controlled its filthy columns."

On a fellow Whig convicted of larceny: "[T]he act of stealing is *Democratic.* In other words, the Man is Whig, but the Measure is Democratic."

On Isham G. Harris, secessionist governor of Tennessee: "His com-plexion is sallow—his eyes are dark and penetrating—a perfect index to the heart of a traitor—with the scowl and frown of a demon resting upon his brow. The study of mischief, and the practice of crime, have brought upon him premature baldness and a grey beard. . . . He chews tobacco rapidly, and is inordinately fond of liquor."

On witnessing a Baptist foot-washing ritual: "Never did I, before or since, see as many big dirty feet, washed in one large pewter basin full of water."

On being asked to serve as a chaplain in the Confederate army: "When I shall have made up my mind to go to hell, I will cut my throat, and go *direct,* and not travel round by way of the Southern Confederacy."[2]

Brownlow's relentless assaults infuriated many of his victims. Few public figures of his era were more deeply loathed by their enemies. A number of the injured replied in kind, though few could trade insults with Brownlow and come out ahead. Some decided that verbal dueling was insufficient to redeem their honor. In the course of his long career the Parson was threatened, sued, beaten up, shot at (and hit once), hanged in effigy, indicted, imprisoned, and even exiled by his adversaries. But such reprisals did not silence him; they merely gave him more ammunition to fire off in his devastating broadsides.

Brownlow directed his fiercest attacks against those who endeavored to break up the Union, and it was to further his antisecession crusade that he brought forth *Parson Brownlow's Book.* He first took a stand on the sectional issue in the early 1830s, when South Carolina tried to nullify a federal law. Though he switched sides on certain other issues over the years, he never renounced his Unionism. His steadfast loyalty to the United States brought him in 1861 to the gravest crisis of his career, and his one moment of real greatness.

As the North-South political conflict intensified in the 1840s and 1850s, the citizens of Tennessee generally took a conservative, centrist position. Thus Brownlow, who blamed radical northern abolitionists and radical southern "fire-eaters" equally for stirring up sectional controversies, was during those years very much in the mainstream of political opinion in his state. Even in the wake of the 1860 election, when Republican Abraham Lincoln of Illinois won the presidency on a free-soil platform and the seven states of the Deep South (led by South Carolina) consequently broke from the Union, Tennesseans on the

2. Sources for the above quotations are as follows: R. B. Lattimore, "A Survey of William G. Brownlow's Criticisms of the Mormons, 1841–1857," *Tennessee Historical Quarterly* 27 (1968): 256 (on Mormons); Steve Humphrey, *"That D———d Brownlow": Being a Saucy and Malicious Description of William Gannaway Brownlow . . .* (Boone, 1978), 85 (on larceny); Robert H. White and Stephen V. Ash, eds., *Messages of the Governors of Tennessee,* 10 vols. to date (Nashville, 1952–), 5:440 (on Harris); E. Merton Coulter, *William G. Brownlow, Fighting Parson of the Southern Highlands* (Chapel Hill, 1937; reprint, Knoxville, 1971), 18, 41, 95, 121, 143–44 (all others).

whole stood with Brownlow in rejecting secession. Only with the bombardment of the U.S. Army's Fort Sumter in Charleston Harbor in April 1861, and Lincoln's subsequent call for troops to suppress the southern "rebellion," did the majority of Tennessee's citizens change their allegiance. Under the leadership of Governor Harris, the state then withdrew from the Union and joined the newly-formed Confederate States of America.

But not all Tennesseans approved. Though secessionism swept Middle and West Tennessee in April, East Tennessee held firm against the tide. In that region, where slaves and plantations were few and the planter aristocracy negligible, the great majority saw no reason to break up the Union merely because a northern Republican was president. Led by Brownlow and Andrew Johnson (now temporarily reconciled) and other prominent loyalists, most East Tennesseans affirmed their fealty and rallied against the Confederacy.

At first Governor Harris and the Confederate authorities tried to conciliate the disaffected East Tennesseans. Their leniency won no converts, however, and eventually they cracked down hard on the defiant Unionists. Brownlow, who had continued to crank out anti-Confederate editorials in the *Whig* after the state's secession, was by December 1861 locked up in the Knoxville jail on a charge of treason. Despite his suffering (vividly described in *Parson Brownlow's Book*— see Part IV within), he refused to take the Confederate oath of allegiance that would have freed him. Instead, he prepared calmly for the hanging he expected, and composed a farewell address to his fellow Unionists.

Brownlow did not hang. The Confederates decided instead to banish him. He was escorted under a flag of truce to the Union army lines in Middle Tennessee and on March 15, 1862, was turned over to U.S. authorities. Following a brief stay in Nashville (which had been captured by the Federal army in February), he headed across the Ohio River to tell his story to northern audiences. After several weeks on the road, speaking to packed houses in Cincinnati, Indianapolis, Chicago, Columbus, Pittsburgh, Philadelphia, and other cities, he settled in New Jersey to compose a book about his experiences.

Brownlow was in a hurry to get his book out so he could resume his speaking tour, and he managed to put the manuscript together in less than a month. Anyone who reads the original can see that it was done in haste. It comprises for the most part editorials and correspondence concerning secession and the war clipped from the pages of the *Whig*. These are strung together with occasional commentary and grouped into eighteen chapters with little thematic coherence or chronological consistency. The latter part of the book is a narrative (in four chapters) of Brownlow's experiences from the time of the Confederate crackdown until his arrival in New Jersey. It includes a diary he kept in jail, correspondence between him and the Confederate authorities in Knoxville and Richmond, and some of his speeches.

Parson Brownlow's Book took the North by storm: an estimated one hundred thousand copies were sold by September 1862. Today's readers, however, would find the book rather rough going. Sections of it are tedious, repetitive, or irrelevant, and it is awkwardly organized. For that reason it seemed better to offer modern readers not the work as originally written but a selection of excerpts carefully chosen and logically arranged.

In the present volume Brownlow's twenty-two chapters have been replaced by four parts. Part I contains his dedication, preface, and autobiographical sketch just as he wrote them; that is, with no deletions. Part II contains editorials, correspondence, speeches, etc., most of which were originally printed in the *Whig*. Those pieces selected for inclusion amount to about one third of the material of that sort in the original book, and they are placed here in chronological order. Part III is an essay on East Tennessee that comprised a single chapter in the original book. It is reprinted here with very minor elisions. Part IV is Brownlow's narrative of his imprisonment and subsequent travels. His original is for the most part left intact, up to the point when he arrived in Nashville; the material on his northern tour, including mostly speeches that merely recapitulate his experiences among the Rebels, has been omitted.[3]

3. I have marked all deletions with ellipsis points. I have modernized Brownlow's punctuation to some extent, but not (except in a few cases) his spelling. I have silently corrected his few misspellings and typographical errors, and have kept annotation to a minimum, inserting it with brackets in Brownlow's text where that could be done unobtrusively, otherwise consigning it to footnotes.

The Parson's book had three purposes. The first was to raise public and official awareness in the North about the plight of the East Tennessee Unionists, who were suffering for their loyalty to the old flag; the Lincoln administration, Brownlow insisted, must make the liberation of East Tennessee from Confederate control a top priority. The second purpose was to raise money to reestablish his newspaper in Knoxville as soon as the town was liberated (the Confederates had confiscated his press and other equipment). His last aim was to discredit the Confederacy by portraying it as a despotism ruled by scheming demagogues and policed by drunks and thugs.

The book's influence on the North cannot be gauged precisely but was certainly substantial; judged on its own terms, it was a resounding success. Some of Brownlow's assertions, however, were misleading. By confirming northern suspicions that secession was the work of a cabal of self-interested southern politicians who had used force, fraud, and deception to achieve their aims, Brownlow encouraged northerners to dismiss the South's very real fears about the survival of slavery and fostered the mistaken belief that the "deluded" southern citizenry needed only a bit of enlightenment and encouragement to bring them to their senses and back into the Union. Too, Brownlow's insistence that a northern army could quickly and easily invade East Tennessee inspired unrealistic hopes and plans in the North.

If Brownlow's book is more propaganda than reasoned and judicious explication, it is nevertheless magnificent propaganda. In its pages the reader will find the inimitable Parson at his best. By turns sarcastic, angry, high-minded, informative, compassionate, and droll, he forthrightly proclaims his convictions and excoriates his foes. Every sentence exemplifies the motto that adorned the masthead of his newspaper: "Cry aloud and spare not."

After turning over his manuscript to the publisher, Brownlow went on the road again to lecture. Early in 1863 he returned to Nashville and took a job as U.S. Treasury agent. In September of that year Yankee troops finally occupied Knoxville; the Parson arrived there hard on their heels. He resurrected his newspaper, renaming it the *Whig and Rebel Ventilator,* and resumed his editorial flogging of the Confederacy. In 1865 a Unionist state government was established in Tennessee, and Brownlow was elected governor. His four-year tenure as Reconstruction governor of the Volunteer State, though not without accomplishments, was as turbulent and controversial as his wartime career. He outraged the former Confederates and even the more conservative Unionists by allying with the Radical Republicans, enfranchising blacks, disfranchising ex-Rebels, and manipulating election returns and voter registration to keep himself in power—all the while denouncing his enemies with his usual vitriol. In 1869 he resigned the governorship to take a seat in the U.S. Senate, where he served until 1875. He died in Knoxville in 1877.

Few historians, in this century at least, have had much good to say about Brownlow, especially concerning his stormy postwar career. Indeed, in a 1981 poll Tennessee historians ranked the Parson dead last among the state's governors. (He scored a 1.63 average on a 10-point scale—far below the next-to-last, Ray Blanton, who went to prison for selling state liquor licenses.)[4]

Perhaps a new generation of historians will one day rehabilitate the reputation of the "Fighting Parson" of East Tennessee. He will probably never win any plaudits for his Machiavellian maneuvering as governor, nor for the petty and often mean partisanship that marked much of his prewar career. But surely it is time to acknowledge Brownlow's noble fortitude in the cause of the Union. Languishing in jail under threat of execution, he defied his captors. Urged by a Rebel general to take a simple oath to the Confederate government and thereby gain his freedom, the Parson practically spit in his face: "I told him that I would lie here until I died with old age before I would take such an oath," reported Brownlow in his book. "I [said I] did not consider that he had a Government; I regarded it as a big Southern mob."

Let us give the Parson his due. Flawed though he was in many ways, for a time in 1861 and 1862 he was a hero; and *Parson Brownlow's Book* is the essential testimony of his patriotic faith.

4. *Tennessee Historical Quarterly* 41(1982):100.

I

DEDICATION, PREFACE, AND AUTOBIOGRAPHICAL SKETCH

TO

✝

Every honest Patriot citizen, and unconditional Union man, who loves Loyalty and despises Rebellion, whether perpetrated North or South, under one pretence or another, for the sake of office, power, fame, money, or malicious resentment; To every intelligent reading man, who, to whatever party he may belong, is unwilling to see his Government overthrown by wicked and designing men, and who has resolved to live and die beneath the folds of the Star-Spangled Banner; To my companions in the Knoxville Jail, who, with me, swore upon the altar of our country that, despite the gallows and the prison, they would adhere to the Flag of the Federal Union, and who look to the mild umpirage of the Union as the only shield of nationality, is this work

DEDICATED BY ITS AUTHOR,

Who, during the progress of this revolution, has opposed it at every step, regardless of consequences personal to himself, and of what designing men might say or think, or of what a corrupt and pensioned Southern Press might charge, as to motives; who still bears in mind that it was WASHINGTON who told us, "THE CONSTITUTION IS SACREDLY OBLIGATORY UPON ALL"; and that it was JACKSON who said, "THE UNION, IT MUST BE PRESERVED!" This is a truth now revealed to us,

> Which kings and prophets waited for,
> And sought, but never found.

PREFACE

†

I have prepared this work from the single stand-point of uncompromising devotion to the American Union as established by our fathers, and unmitigated hostility to the armed rebels who are seeking its destruction. My ancestors fought in its defence; and while their blood flows in my veins I shall instinctively recoil from bartering away the glory of its past and the prophecy of its future for the stained record of that vile thing, begotten by fraud, crime, and bad ambition, christened a Southern Confederacy. I cannot exchange historic renown for disgrace, national honor for infamy, how splendid soever may be the bribe or how violent soever may be the compulsion. This is my faith as an American citizen; and this book will show how sorely it has been put to the test. I claim, however, no merit, further than that arising from the discharge of a simple duty both of religion and patriotism. Thousands of my fellow-citizens have been equally faithful among the faithless. Their sufferings may be conceived from this narrative of my own.

Indeed, it is not from the slightest desire of self-glorification that I have spoken so freely of myself. It would have been sheer affectation of modesty to attempt by circumlocution of speech to do otherwise. For I have, in this matter, rather regarded myself as a type of the large body of loyal people in the border States, and have, accordingly, been the more unreserved, inasmuch as I felt that I might assume to some extent to speak in their behalf. It is important that our countrymen of the North should clearly understand the embarrassing position of this class, and the peculiar privations they have been compelled to undergo. It is chiefly due to them that the battle-field of the Rebellion has not been transferred to Northern homes. Their geographical location and political elements are such that, upon the soil which they inhabit, loyalty and treason have overlapped, and being thus confronted face to face, they have been plunged into all the horrors of discord and anarchy, of divided communities and sundered households. In many respects, however, we of that region do not wholly sympathize with the North any more than with the extreme South. We deprecate alike the fanatical agitators of one section and the Disunion demagogues of the other. I believe I represent the views of multitudes of ever-true and now suffering patriots when I declare that, Southern man and slaveholder as I am, if the South in her madness and folly will force the issue upon the country, of Slavery and no Union, or a Union and no Slavery, I am for the Union, though every other institution in the country perish. I am for sustaining this Union if it shall require "coercion" or "subjugation," or, what is worse, the annihilation of the rebel population of the land. These peculiarities in my position, as an East-Tennessean, it will be seen, have contributed to mould the views which I have expressed.

I am, therefore, prepared to expect that many readers will not concur in all that I have said. But I do verily believe that, as a National man—having had an opportunity, as from an intermediate eminence, to view this question on both sides—and having observed the bearings of the whole subject for thirty years past, I am enabled to suggest something worthy the consideration of my countrymen. Hence I have not consulted the opinions of others, nor reflected whether what I say would be acceptable or unacceptable, would render the writer popular or unpopular. I seek only to utter the profound convictions of my own mind, in order that, God willing, I may be of some benefit in my day and generation, and, without fear or favor, come weal or woe, may have the sad privilege of warning my fellow-citizens, even if I may not enjoy the cheerful satisfaction of convincing them.

I have suffered deeply in person and estate, have avoided no responsibility, have endured evil treatment and imprisonment, and been compelled day by day to contemplate the near prospect of a brutal death upon the gallows—all in behalf of the sacred cause I have espoused. I avouch these things as evidence of sincerity. Not only so, but they have left me in no mood for the use of softened forms of speech in narrating such acts or depicting the actors. Hence I have spoken plainly. Extreme fastidiousness of taste may, perhaps, shrink with over-sensitiveness from some of the language I have employed. But it was no time for dalliance with polished sentences or enticing words; for an imminent necessity—like the "burden" of the old Hebrew prophets—was upon us, and the cause of our LORD and LAND could be best served by the sturdy rhetoric of defiance and the unanswerable logic of facts. The traitors merited a sword-thrust style, and deserved the strongest epithet I have applied. My persecution by them was such that I had a fair right to handle them roughly: they were not worth any other mode of treatment; and I have written what I have written.

I cannot close this preface without expressing my thanks for the generous reception I have met with at the North. In Cincinnati, Columbus, Chicago, Philadelphia, New York—indeed, wherever I have gone—I have been welcomed by individuals and by public bodies with demonstrations of honor and kindness which seem like a providential recompense for all I have endured. I shall preserve a life-long recollection of such universal and spontaneous sympathy, and leave its precious memory and memorials as an heir-loom to the latest generation of my descendants. I bear this testimony all the more willingly, because these courtesies vindicate me from aspersions, and are occasioned by no modification or concealment of my opinions. I have, everywhere, condemned the disorganizing propagandists of the North, and have publicly proclaimed that I was a Southerner by birth, education, and habits; yet, when I also announced that I was a National man and uncompromisingly for the Union, I found that other things were forgotten, and that I had touched a chord which made us all of kin.

God grant that we may, as Sections, Churches, and Individuals, realize how great a share each of us has had in bringing about our present calamities, and, consequently, how much of the responsibility falls upon *self* as well as upon others! When this shall be felt, and when a proper spirit shall accompany the conviction, the horrors of this wicked war will be appreciated, the hand of vengeance will be stayed, and

Returning Justice lift aloft her scale.

W. G. B.

Philadelphia, May, 1862

AUTOBIOGRAPHICAL SKETCH

†

It is a delicate task for a modest man to perform, when he undertakes to write out a memorial of himself, and especially when he shall undertake to give both his *private* and *public* life. But as I have never arisen to any thing like eminence, and as it is the custom of such only as have, to write out a full history of themselves, and to give their *bad* as well as *good* deeds to the world, I will be spared the labor and mortification of any unfavorable disclosures.

It will, perhaps, be urged that *both sides* of a man's picture of life should be given, and then the reader, having the *whole man* before him, will be the better prepared to award to him a righteous verdict. Others will insist that a man should so conduct himself as to be wholly free from improprieties, especially if he be a member of the Church, or wear clerical robes. To this I reply, that if the memoirs of only such as have lived and died without fault, and without incurring the displeasure of designing and bad men, were written, we should seldom, if ever, see a production of the kind.

I lay no claim whatever to *inimitable excellencies*; but I do claim that my good and evil deeds, if placed in a scale, would not be so perfectly poised that neither end would preponderate! An anecdote of my life will illustrate my views of this subject.

Whilst in attendance at an Annual Conference of the Methodist Church, in Abingdon, Virginia, some twelve years ago, I suffered from an attack of fever; and, either from the influence of medicine, or of fever on the brain, I became a little flighty. The opinion prevailed that I would die, and the venerable BISHOP [WILLIAM] CAPERS, and other ministers, became anxious to know how the "eccentric Parson" felt in view of an exchange of worlds. Accordingly, they visited my room, and the Bishop read the Scriptures, and sang and prayed with and for me. On taking his leave of me—holding me by the hand and looking me full in the face—he inquired what my prospects were beyond the grave. It is said—and I have no doubt of the truth of the statement—that I returned for an answer, "Well, Bishop, if I had my life to live over again, I could improve it in many respects, and would try to do so. However, if the books have been properly kept in the other world, *there is a small balance in my favor!*"

I have lived long enough in this present evil world to have enlisted the sympathies of many friends, and at the same time to have excited the bitter resentments of many foes. This affords me proof that I have not been a *negative* character. That a man engaged in the work of propagating Christianity, in opposing error and defending the cause of truth, and, finally, in going about endeavoring to do good, should find himself exposed to enemies, or should meet with violent and protracted opposition, may seem strange. But history and observation inform us that such has been the lot of all *decided* public men, in a greater or less degree. While some emblazon a man's virtues, others will amplify his faults. A majority, however, labor

> The struggling pangs of conscious truth to hide,
> To quench the blushes of ingenuous shame

rather than pursue the opposite course; and it is more than likely that on this account religious sectarians and political partisans have denied me justice. For it has certainly been my lot in life to have the shafts of unmerited censure hurled at me; and since this GREAT REBELLION has been inaugurated, I have been doomed to bear the base insinuations of invidious tongues and pens in Rebeldom!

Perhaps it will be asked, Who is the person that offers this volume to the world? In this the inquisitive reader shall be gratified; for short and simple are the domestic annals of the writer, though in his fifty-seventh year. I am the eldest son of JOSEPH A. BROWNLOW, who was born and raised in Rockbridge county, Virginia, and died in Sullivan county, in East Tennessee, in 1816. My father died when I was so young that I could not have been a judge of his character; but it has been a source of consolation to me to hear him spoken of by his old associates and schoolmates (General SAM HOUSTON among them) as a man of good sense, brave independence, and of sterling integrity. He was a private in a Tennessee company in the War of 1812. Two of his brothers were at the battle of the *Horseshoe [Bend]*, under General [ANDREW] JACKSON, two others of them died naval officers, and their remains sleep in Norfolk and New Orleans.

The death of my father was a grievous affliction to my mother, as she was left with five helpless children—three sons and two daughters—four of whom are now dead, having heard of the death of the last of the four since my banishment from home! My mother's maiden name was CATHARINE GANNAWAY—a Virginian likewise, of respectable parentage, *and slave-owners*.

She departed this transitory life in less than three months after the death of her husband. Being naturally mild and agreeable in her temperament, she was warmly endeared to a large circle of friends and acquaintance. But their consolation was in this, that, while sinking into the cold embrace of death, she was happy in the religion of Christ.

I was born in Wythe county, Virginia, on the 29th of August, 1805. After the death of my parents, I lived with my mother's relations, who raised me up to hard labor, until I was eighteen years old, when I removed to Abingdon, in that State, and served as a regular apprentice to the trade of a house-carpenter. I have been a laboring-man all my life long, and have acted upon the Scriptural maxim of eating my bread in the sweat of my brow. Though a Southern man in feeling and principle, I do not think it *degrading* to a man to labor, as do most of the Southern Disunionists. Whether East or West, North or South, I recognize the *dignity of labor*, and look forward to a day, not very distant, when *educated labor* will be the salvation of this vast country!

My education was imperfect and irregular, even in those branches taught in the common-schools of the country. I labored, after obtaining a trade, until I acquired the means of again going to school. I afterwards entered the Methodist Travelling Ministry, and travelled ten years without intermission. I availed myself of this position to study and improve my limited education, which I did in all the English branches.

I am about six feet high, and have weighed as heavy as one hundred and seventy-five pounds—have had as fine a constitution as any man need desire. I have very few gray hairs in my head, and, although rather *hard-favored* than otherwise, I will pass for a man of forty years. I have had as strong a voice as any man in East Tennessee, where I have resided for the last thirty years, and have a family of seven children. I have been speaking all that time; and for the last twenty-five years I have edited and published a WHIG newspaper having a larger circulation than any political paper in the State, and even larger than all the papers in East Tennessee put together. I have taken a part in all the religious and political controversies of my day and time.

I have written several books; but the one which has had the largest run is the one entitled, *The [Great] Iron Wheel Examined; [or,] Its False Spokes Extracted*—being a vindication of the Methodist Church against the attacks of Rev. J. R. GRAVES, of Nashville. My reply was published by the Southern Methodist Publishing House, and at the earnest solicitation of the book-agents and other leading members of the Church. It is a work of great severity, but was written in reply to one of still greater severity.

In September, 1858, I was engaged in a debate upon the Slavery question, in Philadelphia, with Rev. ABRA[HA]M PRYNE, of New York, in which I defended the institution of Slavery as it exists in the South. The debate was published in Philadelphia, and exhibits my sentiments upon that great question, which have undergone no change since then.

I am known throughout the length and breadth of the land as the "Fighting Parson"; while I may say, without incurring the charge of egotism, that no man is more peaceable, as my neighbors will testify. Always poor, and always oppressed with *security* debts, few men in my section and of my limited means have given away more in the course of each year to charitable objects. I have never been arraigned in the Church for any immorality. I never played a card. I never was a profane swearer. I never drank a dram of liquor, until within a few years—when it was taken as a medicine. I never had a cigar or chew of tobacco in my mouth. I never was in attendance at a theatre. I never attended a horse-race, and never witnessed their running, save on the fair-grounds of my own county. I never courted but one woman; and her I married.

I may be allowed to say that I have ever been, as I still am, quite a politician, though I have never been an office-seeker[1] nor an office-holder. I began my political career in Tennessee in 1828, by espousing the cause of JOHN QUINCY ADAMS as against ANDREW JACKSON. The latter I regard as having been a true patriot and a sincere lover of his country. The former I admired because he was a learned statesman, of pure moral and private character, and because I regarded him as a FEDERALIST, representing my political opinions. I have all my life long been a FEDERAL WHIG of the WASHINGTON AND ALEXANDER HAMILTON school. I am the advocate of a *concentrated* Federal Government, or of a strong *central* Government, able to maintain its dignity, to assert its authority, and to crush out any rebellion that may be inaugurated. I have never been a *Sectional*, but at all times a *National* man, supporting men for the Presidency and Vice-Presidency without any regard on which side of Mason & Dixon's Line they were born, or resided at the time of their nomination. In a word, I am, as I ever have been, an ardent WHIG, and [HENRY] CLAY and [DANIEL] WEBSTER have ever been my standards of political orthodoxy. With the breaking up of old parties, I have merged every thing into the great question of the "Union, the Constitution, and the Enforcement of the Laws." Hence, I am an *unconditional* Union man, and advocate the preservation of the Union at the expense of all other considerations.

1. Though the Parson did not regard himself as an "office-seeker," he had in fact run for office at least twice. In 1845 he unsuccessfully challenged Andrew Johnson for a congressional seat; and in 1861 he conducted a halfhearted, and likewise unsuccessful, campaign for the governorship (see his announcement of March 23, 1861, in Part II within).

II

EDITORIALS, CORRESPONDENCE,
SPEECHES, ETC.

†

REMARKS DURING DEBATE, PHILADELPHIA, SEPTEMBER 11, 1858

Who can estimate the value of the American Union? Proud, happy, thrice-happy America! The home of the oppressed, the asylum of the emigrant! where the citizen of every clime, and the child of every creed, roam free and untrammelled as the wild winds of heaven! Baptized at the fount of Liberty in fire and blood, cold must be the heart that thrills not at the name of the American Union! When the Old World, with "all its pomp, and pride, and circumstance," shall be covered with oblivion—when thrones shall have crumbled and dynasties shall have been forgotten—may this glorious Union, *despite the mad schemes of Southern fire-eaters and Northern Abolitionists*—stand amid regal ruin and national desolation, towering sublime, like the last mountain in the Deluge—majestic, immutable, and magnificent!

In pursuance of this, let every conservative Northern man, who loves his country and her institutions, shake off the trammels of Northern fanaticism, and swear upon the altar of his country that he will stand by her Constitution and laws. Let every Southern man shake off the trammels of *disunion* and *nullification*, and pledge his life and his sacred honor to stand by the Constitution of his country *as it is*, the laws as enacted by Congress and interpreted by the Supreme Court. Then we shall see every heart a shield, and a drawn sword in every hand, to preserve the ark of our political safety! Then we shall see reared a fabric upon our national Constitution, which time cannot crumble, persecution shake, fanaticism disturb, nor revolution change, but which shall stand among us like some lofty and stupendous Apennine, while the earth rocks at its feet, and the thunder peals above its head!

Camden, Ark., June 30, 1860

W. G. BROWNLOW:

I have learned with pleasure, upon what I consider reliable authority, that you have made up your mind to join the Democratic party, and in future to act with us for the benefit of the country. When will you come out and announce it? It will have a good effect in the present election, if you will make it known over your own signature. Hoping to hear from you, I am, very truly,

JORDAN CLARK

Knoxville, August 6, 1860

MR. JORDAN CLARK:

I have your letter of the 30th ult., and hasten to let you know the *precise time* when I expect to come out and formally announce that I have joined the Democratic party. When the sun shines at midnight and the moon at mid-day; when man forgets to be selfish, or Democrats lose their inclination to steal; when nature stops her onward march to rest, or all the water-courses in America flow up stream; when flowers lose their odor, and trees shed no leaves; when birds talk, and beasts of burden laugh; when damned spirits swap hell for heaven with the angels of light, and pay them the boot in mean whiskey; when impossibilities are in fashion, and no proposition is too absurd to be believed—you may credit the report that I have joined the Democrats!

I join the Democrats! Never, so long as there are sects in churches, weeds in gardens, fleas in hog-pens, dirt in victuals, disputes in families, wars with nations, water in the ocean, bad men in America, or base women in France! No, Jordan Clark, you may hope, you may congratulate, you may reason, you may sneer, but that cannot be. The thrones of the Old World, the courts of the universe, the governments of the world, may all fall and crumble into ruin—the New World may commit the national suicide of dissolving this Union—but all this, and more, must occur before I join the Democracy!

I join the Democracy! Jordan Clark, you know not what you say. When I join the Democracy, the Pope of Rome will join the Methodist Church. When Jordan Clark, of Arkansas, is President of the Republic of Great Britain by the universal suffrage of a contented people; when Queen Victoria consents to be divorced from Prince Albert by a county court in Kansas; when Congress obliges, by law, James Buchanan to marry a European princess; when the Pope leases the Capitol at Washington for his city residence; when Alexander of Russia and Napoleon of France are elected Senators in Congress from New Mexico; when good men cease to go to heaven, or bad men to hell; when this world is turned upside down; when proof is afforded, both clear and unquestionable, that there is no God; when men turn to ants, and ants to elephants—I will change my political faith and come out on the side of Democracy!

Supposing that this full and frank letter will enable you to fix upon *the period* when I will come out a full-grown Democrat, and to communicate the same to all whom it may concern in Arkansas,

I have the honor to be, &c.,

W. G. Brownlow

Editorial, November 10, 1860[1]

With all our progressive developments in the South—and we hail them all with pleasure—still are we, *ex necessitate rei* [i.e., by necessity], largely dependent upon the mind and labor of the North. If this dependence be a sin, as Southern fire-eaters contend it is, how deeply we are all involved in transgression! The very knives and combs in our pockets, the hats upon our heads, the shoes upon our feet, the clothes upon our backs, the razors with which we shave, the cologne with which we perfume our hair, to say nothing of the furniture of our parlors, the ware upon our tables, the implements of husbandry in our fields, the coffins in which we are buried, the spades with which our graves are dug—all come from the North, and will rise up and condemn us. When we have erected manufacturing establishments, and applauded them as Southern enterprises, the truth still stares us all in

---

1. The date is incorrectly given as 1861 in Brownlow's original text.

the face that they have nevertheless been inaugurated by Northern genius, supplied by Northern machinery, and worked by Northern men. The very *types* on which the South is dependent for the issue of her scores of newspapers and periodicals, as well as our printing-presses and ink, to black these types, come from the North! While, therefore, we consent to share the *shame* of this our humiliating dependency, let us be a little more slow to censure harshly the noble enterprise of our neighbors beyond the Potomac, and equally so to anathematize our Southern neighbors who deal with them, until we provide at home the *necessaries* of both life and death.

When South Carolina goes out of the Union, and a few other "Cotton States" follow her iniquitous example, where will they get shoes and coarse clothes for their negroes? Where will they get types and presses to print their fire-eating journals and doctrines? The truth is, we are acting the fool at the South, and the Abolitionists are playing the same game at the North. We can't do without their productions, and they can't do without our rice, sugar, and cotton. Had we not, then, better "live and let live"?[2]

Editorial, November 24, 1860[3]

It is ascertained, beyond controversy, that Mr. LINCOLN is President of the United States. And at a moment when a fierce struggle is going on between passion and reason, we propose, in a spirit of patriotism and compromise, to submit a few leading facts for the consideration of conservative men in the South. We are not so vain as to suppose that what we can say will stay the tide of passion in certain quarters in the South, and bring back the impetuous wanderers to consider great facts and principles. Yet the task of *trying* even those of our countrymen ought not to be shrunk from by conservative and patriotic men of the South,

---

2. A few times Brownlow edited previously published material before putting it into his book, usually with the intention of rendering his remarks less offensive to his northern audience. Here is one instance. As printed in the *Whig*, this editorial had a third paragraph asserting that the South actually had (thanks to its staple exports, which northern industry and commerce greatly depended on) the economic power to dominate the North, but had failed to exercise that power.

3. The date is incorrectly given as November 17 in Brownlow's original text.

whose Southern birth and raising, and long services in behalf of the Union and the maintenance of the laws, may be urged as a reason why they are at least entitled to a patient and respectful hearing. It is an ungracious and thankless task to exhort the LEADERS of the Breckinridge[4] party in South Carolina, Georgia, Florida, Virginia, Alabama, and Mississippi, to calmness, or to a patriotic reconsideration of the perilous position to which, under the apprehensions engendered by the election of a Northern Sectional President, they are plunging under the impulses of passion.

The fact which stares us in the face, and which all parties have to meet, whether they support Bell, Douglas, or Breckinridge, is Mr. Lincoln's election. Mr. Lincoln himself is no doubt a patriotic man, and a sincere lover of his country. He is to-day, what he has always been, an OLD CLAY WHIG, differing in no respect—not even upon the subject of *Slavery*—from the Sage of Ashland. The great objection with us to his election is the *sectional idea* upon which he was run, the *character of the partisans* who supported him and will, it is to be feared, to some extent control his administration. But Lincoln is chosen President, and, whether with or without the consent and participation of the South, will be, and *ought* to be, inaugurated on the 4th of March, 1861. True, as the lights before us indicate, we should say that Lincoln has not received more than one-third to two-fifths of the aggregate vote of the nation. Neither did Buchanan; and yet he, like Lincoln, has been elected by divisions among his opponents. Lincoln, then, has been chosen legally and constitutionally, without either fraud or violence, simply by the suffrages of an enormous majority of the people of the North, who have actually given him more Electoral votes than Buchanan received, who was permitted quietly to take his seat. Against the *manner* of his election nothing can be urged. It is true, as we have before stated, he was a *sectional* candidate; and it is equally true that, with trifling exceptions in Maryland, Virginia, Kentucky, and Mis-

4. Four men vied for the presidency in the 1860 election. John C. Breckinridge was the southern Democratic candidate and the favorite of the more radical southern-rights advocates. Stephen A. Douglas was the northern Democratic candidate, and Abraham Lincoln was the Republican. Brownlow supported John Bell of the Constitutional Union party, who appealed mainly to the conservative ex-Whigs of the Upper South.

souri, he received no Southern votes. But do the Constitution or the laws of our country require a man to receive Southern votes before he can be inaugurated President? Do they compel a candidate to receive votes in *every State* before he shall be declared our Chief Magistrate? Certainly not. Then there is no just ground for resistance or revolutionary movement on that score.

But the argument of Secessionists is, that the administration of a Black Republican[5] President must necessarily be of an aggressive character towards the South, and that the Slave States should forestall such iniquitous policy by withdrawing from the Union. Nay, the election of a man to the Presidency by a party known to be opposed to slavery, and who heretofore have never been successful in such a contest, is alleged to be a just cause for secession. This view of the subject is so fallacious, and so extremely shallow, that it ought not to mislead any one. The argument is, that the South is exposed to all the wiles and infamy of an Abolition Government—an argument that we cannot accept as legitimate in fact or in reason. Did Lincoln receive the suffrages of the North under a pledge that, if elected, he would disregard his oath of office, violate the Constitution, and subvert the Union? Certainly not; for had he given that pledge, the day his election was announced, the entire South would have been united in carrying out a most thorough and determined revolution, and thousands of true men at the North would have joined us. But, now that Lincoln is elected, will he execute the purposes of Abolitionism? This he cannot do under the solemn oath to be administered at his inauguration. And who will say that he intends taking that oath with treason in his heart and perjury on his tongue? We have no right to judge of Lincoln by any thing but his *acts*, and these can only be appreciated *after* his inauguration. He knows very well that he cannot violate the Constitution in any serious particular, without rendering the dissolution of the Union necessary on the part of the South, and thereby involving the North in alarming troubles and certain ruin. The Constitution was planned by its sagacious and patriotic authors to protect the South in just such an emer-

5. "Black Republican," a favorite epithet of southerners, alluded not to race or color but to the antislavery stance of the Republican party.

gency as this. If, then, Lincoln is not a patriot at *heart*—and we assume no such thing—the Constitution and his oath will make him administer the Government *patriotically.*

But the attempt to break up the Union, before awaiting a single overt act, or even the manifestation of the purpose of the President elect, would be wicked, treacherous, unjustifiable, unprecedented, and without the shadow of an excuse. And then, again, disunion is not a remedy for any evil in the Government, real or imaginary; and it is an uncertain and a perilous remedy, to be resorted to only in the last extremity, and as a refuge from wrongs more intolerable than the desperate remedy by which they are sought to be relieved. What the people of the Southern States should do may be summed up in a single word: PAUSE! It will be time enough to fight Lincoln with powder and sword—to resist him with regiments of "minute-men"—when we find that constitutional resistance fails, or that he and his party are bent on our humiliation and destruction. Let every man in every Southern State stand up for the Union as long as it is possible to prevent it. *Individually*, we are willing to go with the South, *even unto death*, but we feel bound to aid in making the South herself *go right!* Let all patriots, irrespective of parties, choose their position; let them resolve to stand by the Union as long as the Federal Government respects the rights of the people of the South. The Constitutional Union men of the South are largely in the majority, and they are pledged to the support of the rights and honor of the South as well as of the Union, and the maintenance of the spirit and form of our Government. They cannot do less; and they ask their *extreme* brethren to meet them upon a common basis and labor for the accomplishment of a common end.

They ask it in a spirit of mutual toleration, and they concede to thousands of others, who are shaping a different course, the same integrity of purpose, patriotism, and honor which they claim for themselves. Let the entire South unite with the thousands of conservative men North, bury their feuds, make common cause, and in 1864 the National Constitutional men of the country, North, South, East, and West, will overthrow the Sectionalists, and restore the Government to a better condition than it has been in for a quarter of a century. The night is dark, we confess, and troubled, but there are gleams of light along the line of the horizon. Lincoln is President; but he is nothing more. We trust that he contemplates no mischief, but, if he does, he can do none. The Senate, the House of Representatives, and the Supreme Court will hold him in check, and stand by the Constitution and the rights of all sections. Here, then, is our hope, and here is the platform that all conservative men should occupy, and time and reflection will, anon, inspire a sober second thought in quarters where at this moment the blind impulses of passion bear sway. The wise, the safe, and the only honorable course to pursue is pointed out in the following advice by the immortal author of the Declaration of American Independence. Here are his memorable words:

> We must have patience and long endurance, then, with our brethren while under delusion. Give them time for reflection and experience of consequences; keep ourselves in a situation to profit by the chapter of accidents, and separate from our companions only when the sole alternatives left are the dissolution of our Union with them, or submission to a Government without limitation of powers.

There is one other consideration we wish to lay before the calm and considerate men of the South, and that is the division of power between the North and South since the organization of the Government. . . . [T]he South, though always in the minority, from the origin of the Government down to the 4th of March, 1861, has held the Presidency forty-eight years out of seventy-two. The North, on the other hand, has held it twenty-four years—only one-third of the time! Let us do as we would be done by. True, it will be said that the South never furnished a *sectional*, but always a *national*, President. Those now complaining and threatening to go out of the Union have presented a *sectional* man, as much so as Lincoln is; and this cannot be denied!

Editorial, December 22, 1860

The Governor has issued a call for the meeting of the Legislature on Monday, the 7th of January, and that body will call a Convention of the State, to act upon the great and only issue of the day—the breaking up of this Union by the secession of certain States from the Confederacy [i.e., United States]. We shall then be called upon to elect men from all of our Legislative districts, Representative and Senatorial, to represent us in that Convention; and this election will be upon us in a very short time, say two or three months. The single issue will then be *secession or no secession*; or, in other words, *Shall Tennessee follow the Cotton States out of the Union, or remain in the Union, true to the Constitution and the laws?* Let those who dare to favor disunion become candidates, and show their hands. They will not be allowed to dodge the issue: they must declare either *for* or *against* secession. The people will force every man to define his position. We desire to see a candidate in every county on each side of the question, so as fully to test it; and we hope to see the ablest men in the State in the field, on both tickets. It will not be Whig and Democrat, Bell and Breckinridge, or Douglas, but *Union or Disunion*.

The Cotton States have spurned the offer of certain border States to meet them in a friendly conference—declare they are going rashly and headlong out of the Union, and that these border States may either follow them or remain where they are. They allege our unity of *interests*, but refuse us harmony of *action*. Five refractory States claim the right to dictate to TEN conservative States, and to involve them in all the horrors of civil war, extending along a border of fifteen hundred miles; but they indignantly refuse to confer with these TEN States. If these border States were their *enemies*, then there would be some propriety in refusing their *counsels*. The border States have been their *friends*, through evil and good report; they have been their companions in arms, and side by side they have fought many a battle and triumphed over the British and Indians. But *now*, in matters in which we are as deeply interested as they are, they give us the cold shoulder, and refuse to meet us in counsel, to see if some course of procedure cannot be agreed upon by which *all* who are identified in interest should unite forces against our enemies.

We are, in fact, "in the midst of a revolution"—a phrase whose dreadful meaning, as interpreted in the history of nations, none of us now realize the force of. The honest yeomanry of these border States, whose families live by their hard licks, four-fifths of whom own no negroes and never expect to own any, are to be drafted—forced to leave their wives and children to toil and suffer, while they fight for the purse-proud aristocrats of the Cotton States, whose pecuniary abilities will enable them to hire substitutes! Revolution, or civil war, is no *holiday affair*; and those who expect to carry it on by the bright and shining light of pleasure and prosperity are to experience the saddest of disappointments.

Let us be calm, fellow-countrymen of the border States, and weigh well every step we take towards meeting these avowed enemies of the Union in counsel. That great teacher—history—shows a multitude of cases in which whole communities, and sometimes nations, have been led into disastrous and wholesale calamities, under excitements not so terrific as that which now agitates these States. In proof of this, we could refer to the South-Carolina-like insanity which seized upon whole nations of Europe, and led them to inhospitable graves on the bloody fields of battle. The most impressive and notable of these is furnished by the terrific French Revolution, which *began with a Convention*, culminated in the decapitation of a king, and ended in the worst form of a military despotism. Tennesseans! let us not disregard these stern teachings of history. Human nature and man are essentially the same in all ages. The demagogues who denied to us before the late Presidential election that they were at all favorable to Secession, now make light of, and affect to despise, the dangers which are only a few brief months ahead of us. We are urged to go into a Southern Confederacy at once; and in a few months thereafter we shall be drafted as soldiers, and forced to abandon our peaceful homes, never to see them more, to perish by exposure, or hunger, or disease, on long and dreary marches, or to fall by the hands of our countrymen, in a war that never ought to have been waged. This dreadful state of things is just before us in the portentous future, and we are rushing into the jaws of death, led on by the *ignis-fatuus* [i.e, will-o'-the-wisp] of the wild and visionary theorists of the South, who believe that the chief end of man is *nigger!*

But it is said that five or six Cotton States will go out of the Union, and we of the border States will be forced to follow. We say, Let them go, if they are bent upon self-destruction, but let us, Tennesseans, remain in the Union, whose Constitution and laws *provide adequate protection to the rights of all the States of the Confederacy*; and let us look to that instrument for defence *within* the Union, warned by the experience of the past, the dangers of the present, and the hopes of the future. It is worse than idle—it is fool-hardy—to discuss the question of the relative merits of the two Governments, the new and the old. The *spirit* manifested by the Disunionists of the South shows most clearly that they are not the men to make laws for our Government, or to frame a Government for conservative Union men to live under. We may as well live under the government of the *William L. Garrisons* of the North, as the *William L. Yanceys* of the South.[6] In case of disruption, the formation of a Southern Confederacy, by direct taxation, by means of military encampments, and by calling off the yeomanry of the country from agricultural pursuits, will involve us all in one common ruin, in financial embarrassments, and in the overthrow of the best Government the world ever knew. One can but involuntarily turn even from the contemplation of this state of things. Shall we be precipitated into this dreadful state of things by a set of men who denied to us, but three months ago, that they favored Disunion, because they then wanted our votes? If time were given to the North, she would do the South justice: therefore let these border States be guided by moderation. Let us, Tennesseans, stand by the Union; let us hope on, and when hope is gone—so far as we are concerned—life will have lost its value for us![7]

Editorial, January 5, 1861[8]

Seeing that the Episcopal Bishops of the Carolinas have composed prayers to be used by their clergy during the sessions of their Legislatures, we have deemed it proper, sustaining the relation to the Meth-

6. Garrison, of Massachusetts, was among the most radical of abolitionists; Yancey, of Alabama, was a leading secessionist.

7. What the Tennessee legislature actually did after convening on January 7, 1861, was to call for a popular referendum on the question of whether to hold a convention to consider secession. On February 9, Tennesseans went to the polls and by a 55 to 45 percent margin voted "no convention." The simultaneous balloting for delegates to the proposed convention (mandated by the legislature so that, if the convention was approved, a second election would be unnecessary) was even more lopsided: Unionist candidates won 78 percent of the vote, secessionists 22.

8. The date is incorrectly given as 1860 in Brownlow's original text.

odist Church we do in East Tennessee, to compose the following prayer, and order that it shall be used this winter by all *local* preachers in all their public ministrations:

ALMIGHTY GOD, our heavenly Father, in whose hands are the hearts of men, and the issues of events, not mixed up with Locofocoism,[9] nor rendered offensive in Thy sight by being identified with men of corrupt minds, evil designs, and damnable purposes, such as are seeking to up-turn the best form of government on earth, Thou hast graciously promised to hear the prayers of those who in an humble spirit, and with true faith—such as no *Secessionist* can bring into exercise—call upon Thee. Be pleased, we beseech Thee, favorably to look upon and bless the Union men of this Commonwealth, and sustain them in their praiseworthy efforts to perpetuate this Government, and, under it, the institutions of our holy religion. Possess their minds with the spirit of true patriotism, enlightened wisdom, and of persevering hostility towards those traitors, political gamblers, and selfish demagogues who are seeking to build up a miserable Southern Confederacy, and under it to inaugurate a new reading of the Ten Commandments, so as to teach that the *chief end of Man is Nigger!* In these days of trouble and perplexity, give the common people grace to perceive the right path, which, Thou knowest, leads from the camps of Southern mad-caps and Northern fanatics, and enable them steadfastly to walk therein!

So strengthen the common masses, O Lord, and so direct them, that they being hindered neither by the fear of fire-eaters, nor by the love of the corrupt men in power, nor by bribery, nor by an overcharge of mean whiskey, nor by any other *Democratic* passion, but being mindful of Thy constant superintendence, of the awful majesty of Thy righteousness, of Thy hatred of a corrupt Democracy and its profligate leaders, and of the strict account they must hereafter give to Thee, they may, in counsel, word, and deed, aim supremely at the fulfilment of their duty, which is to talk, vote, and pray against the wicked leaders of Abolitionism and the equally ungodly advocates of Secessionism. Grant that those of Thy professed ministers who are mixed up with

9. Brownlow used "Locofoco" (sometimes abbreviated "Loco") as a pejorative term for "Democrat."

modern Democracy, and have become so hardened in sin as openly to advocate the vile delusion, may speedily abandon their *un*ministerial habits, or go over to the cause of the devil, that their positions may at least be unequivocal, and that they may thereby advance the welfare of the country! And grant that these fire-eaters may soon run their race, that the course of this world may be so peaceably ordered, by Thy superintendence, that Thy Church, and Thy whole people, irrespective of sects, may joyfully serve Thee, in all godly quietness, through Jesus Christ our Lord. *Amen!*

Correspondence, 1861

Covington, [Ga.,] Jan. 8, 1861

Brother Brownlow:

Having been a subscriber to your *once readable* paper for a goodly number of years, and having through the agency of its columns formed an opinion of your character which I must in candor own was favorable, I take the privilege which my age, experience, and position in society afford me, to *advise, entreat*, and *warn* you of your approaching danger. Among the most important things in which we have noticed your deviation from the path of rectitude is, that in this present political commotion you have *dabbled* more than becomes you. From all appearances, you have turned from a *private* and *respected citizen* to a *contentious, quarrelsome* politician—from a Southern-Rights man to a friend of the North—from a *Union* man to a *Secessionist*.[10] Can these charges be true? Am I not deceived? I hope so. Yet these reports come from every quarter, and are strengthened by the *tone* of your paper. With you alone, my dear brother, it remains to refute them by your future conduct. These remarks are prompted by a generous heart, and the feeling that causes a friend to inform another of his errors, hoping thereby to correct them. We will close, as "a word to the wise is sufficient." That a speedy reformation may take place, is the wish of

Your affectionate friend,

George P. Nickols

10. Like many other southern-rights advocates, Nickols accused conservatives such as Brownlow of siding with northern sectionalists and thus being "disunionists."

Corinth, Miss., Jan. 10, 1861

Mr. Brownlow, of the United States of America:

I see, in a late issue of your dirty sheet, that you are full of braggado-
cio, and that you declare positively that if Tennessee, and the South
generally, secede, you will still cling to that most abominable of all
abominations, the Union. Now, Parson, if you adopt this policy, what
do you think will be the consequence? You will certainly be hung, as
all dogs should be, until you are "dead, dead." Your crime will be treason of the deepest dye.

I have never believed you to be a Southern man, but a shrewd,
money-making Yankee; and, if you will give me time, I will look into
your nativity. When Tennessee secedes, I will head a company of Tennesseans and Mississippians and proceed to hang you by law, or by
force if need be. The South can look upon you in no other light than
as a traitor and a Tory, and the twin brother of *Andrew Johnson.* Remember, and beware, you shall be hung in the year 1861, unless you
conclude to live the life of an exile.

Yours, &c.,

W. M. Yancey

Knoxville, Jan. 15, 1861

Matchless Sirs:

In a brief reply to your letters, I will first correct the error into which
one of you has fallen as it regards my nativity, &c. I am not "a shrewd,
money-making Yankee," nor am I a money-making man at all—never
was. My town-property and printing-office I estimate to be worth
about *ten thousand dollars.* This is all I have, and is fully as much as I
ever did own at any one time. I am, therefore, a poor man, and never
expect to be any thing else. It would have been otherwise with me, if I
had not *given away* half of all I ever did make, and if I had *sought* to
make money.

As it regards my nativity, I was born and raised in Wythe county,
Virginia, and my parents were both natives of the same State. I have
lived in East Tennessee for thirty years; and, although I am now fifty-
five years of age, I walk erect, have but few gray hairs, and *look* to
be younger than any whiskey-drinking, tobacco-chewing, profane-
swearing Secessionist in any of the Cotton States, of forty years.

As it regards your threats (and both of your letters are of a threatening character), they have no terrors for me. I have no doubt but there are thousands of Secessionists in the South who would be willing to see me hung, and would assist in swinging me up, could they have the slightest pretext for so doing, and meet with an opportunity. When you come to East Tennessee, with a company of Tennesseans, Mississippians, and Georgians, to hang me, please give me ten days' notice, and I will muster men enough in the county where I reside, to hang the last rascal among you, and then use your carcasses for wolf-bait!

This whole scheme of Secession is the most wicked, diabolical, and infernal scheme ever set on foot for the ruin of any country. It has long been contemplated by the Tory leaders of the Cotton States, and the details of it, I see, have just come to light through the *National Intelligencer*, one of the most reliable journals in America. The scheme to avoid a collision about the [tariff] revenue, is to declare Southern ports free to the commerce of the world, raise their revenues by direct taxation and forced loans, and leave the United States and foreign Governments to fight out the question of the collection of the [tariff] revenue. Another one of their schemes was to seize upon all the [U.S. Army] forts and Southern fortifications along the entire coast from Maryland to Texas; and this, like lawless rebels, they have been doing, even before they have seceded. This was all agreed upon before the Charleston Convention, and a part of the programme was to break it up in a row, and prevent the nomination of Douglas, for if nominated they knew he could be elected, and this would prolong the existence of "that most abominable of all abominations, the Union," at least four years longer.[11]

South Carolina, Alabama, Mississippi, and Florida have actually gone out of the Union, and Georgia, Louisiana, Arkansas, and Texas will soon follow. The first four States named have passed their Ordinances of Secession, and published them to the world. They call them *ordinances*; I call them so many covenants with death and agreements

11. The national Democratic convention was held in Charleston, South Carolina, in April 1860. Unable to agree on a presidential candidate, the delegates adjourned and reconvened in Baltimore. Still unable to agree, northern and southern Democrats wound up nominating separate candidates.

with hell! They are so many decrees to carry out the behests of *madmen* and *traitors*. Each ordinance is the twin sister of treason—"treason *de facto*." O Secessionism! "hell is moved at thy coming"; for hell and its infinitely infernal Government are thy offspring. The fallen angels were the first seceders from Paradise, and declared their *"independence"* by promulgating an ordinance in "a lake that burns with fire and brimstone," and "where there is weeping, wailing, and gnashing of teeth; and where the smoke of their torment ascends up for ever and ever"—the reward of their treason being "eternal damnation."

But war has commenced. The first guns have been fired—and fired by South Carolina rebels upon unoffending American soldiers sailing into port under the Stars and Stripes of their country.[12] In four of the States of this Confederacy rebellion bids defiance to law, and "bloody treason flourishes over us." Throughout these four States, judgment and truth seem to have "fled to brutish beasts, and men have lost their reason." Even in the halls of our national Capitol traitors stalk unblushingly, and openly proclaim their treason, denouncing the Government and declaring their purpose to destroy it. Traitors stand on the floor of the American Senate and receive nine dollars per day for proclaiming treason, rank and damning—for which they ought to be hung, and would be if the laws of the land were enforced.

Every man who is worthy of the name of an American citizen will denounce this treason, and rally to the defence of our Constitution and laws. They are the bonds of our Union, and around that Union cluster the hallowed memories of the past and the brightest hopes and dearest interests of the future. Blood, it is plain to be seen, will be shed in its defence; but upon these Secession aggressors be the consequences and responsibilities.

I am for my country, and on the side of the General Government; and in every contest, either at sea or on land, I shall rejoice in the triumph of the Government troops fighting under the Stars and Stripes. Should Tennessee go out of the Union, I shall continue to denounce Secessionism, and war against the storms of fanaticism at the North

12. On January 9, 1861, South Carolina artillery in Charleston harbor fired on and turned back an unarmed steamer, the *Star of the West*, which was attempting to reinforce and resupply the U.S. Army garrison at Fort Sumter.

and the assaults of demagogues and traitors at the South, though their number be legion. In all candor, I believe that in a Southern Confederacy the freedom of speech and of the press will be denied; and for the exercise of them I will be hung. But, come what may, through weal or woe, in peace or war, no earthly power shall keep me from denouncing the enemies of my country until my tongue and pen are paralyzed in death! Once destroyed, this Union can never be reconstructed. And, with others, I have resolved that no earthly power shall prevail against it; that it shall be "perpetual," as our fathers intended it—"one and indivisible, now and forever."

W. G. BROWNLOW

CORRESPONDENCE, 1861

Abbeville C[ourt] H[ouse], S.C., Jan. 27, 1861

W. G. BROWNLOW:

SIR: I wrote to you a few days ago under the signature of "T.J.C.," and informed you that you were the greatest liar out of hell, and one of the most infamous scoundrels living between heaven and earth; and I then told you, and now repeat, that nothing would afford us as much pleasure as to see you in Abbeville, where we could treat you to a coat of tar and feathers. I told you in that brief letter that my understanding was that the people of Knoxville were a respectable and intelligent people, and that it was a matter of surprise that they would allow you to remain in their midst—a vile scamp, as you have shown yourself to be.

Since writing that note to you, I have seen a long and interesting letter from Knoxville to a citizen of this Republic, giving some facts in regard to you that I am resolved the world shall know, at least to the extent of the circulation of Southern papers. I was permitted to take down the *points* made against you in the Knoxville letter, and they are as follows:

1. The Southern States having withdrawn their patronage from your Abolition sheet, you no longer have subscribers enough to defray the expenses of publication, and you are about to starve out.

2. The town and county in which you publish your slanderous sheet

will shortly cast a majority of their votes for Secession, and so will your State.

3. You have repeatedly thrust yourself forward as a candidate for office, but never have been elected.

4. You are indebted to every store in your town—and nothing can be made out of you at law—until you cannot get credit in any store for a suit of clothes!

5. Your own partisans refuse, upon the stump, to endorse any thing you say, and will not be held to an account for your doctrines; while the common people send off to other sections of your State for newspapers.

6. The members of your Church have no respect for you, and the better class refuse to speak to you, either publicly or privately.

This, you lying old hypocrite, is your character furnished by a South Carolinian from your own town, where you are best known.

T. J. Cinclair

Knoxville, Feb. 14, 1861

T. J. Cinclair:

Your insulting letter is before me, and I take the opportunity to reply, though I have no idea that I am replying to a *gentleman*, or a man who pays his just debts, or tells the truth in common conversation. I am not ignorant of the deadly opposition to me in South Carolina, and more especially from the blackguard portion of her citizens, of whom *you* are a fit representative. I expect that the vials of contumely, reproach, and defamation will be poured upon me by a hireling press of a corrupt and plundering Southern Confederacy, by the insolvent bullies, hardened liars, and vulgar cut-throats whose only ambition is to serve as tools under an arrogant and hateful pack of aristocratic leaders. But while I have strength to wield a pen, my nerve shall be exerted in defence of that *Union* which was purchased with blood. Under the mantle of freedom, dark assassins of our National Constitution are endeavoring to insinuate themselves into the temple of those privileges, our rights to which were secured by the toil of our fathers and sealed with their blood. But these border States will teach you that our Constitution is not built upon such a sandy foundation as to be shaken and demolished without the rotten pillar of reputed South Carolina orthodoxy to support it.

As it regards your Knoxville letter-writer, he is a *liar* and a *coward*, and *dare* not give his name to the public. My neighbors, without distinction of parties, will testify that he is a liar. Even my *enemies*—and I have some—will testify from their own personal knowledge that he is a liar. I do not believe, for one moment, that any citizen of Knoxville ever wrote any such letter to South Carolina. You have been duped for once, or else some straggling subject of your contemptible Southern Confederacy has passed through here and sent to your would-be Republic the infinitely infernal production from which you quote your six propositions.

I would as soon be engaged in importing the plague from the East, as in helping to build up a Southern Confederacy upon the ruins of the American Constitution. I expect to be abused for my defence of the Union. "Tray, Blanche, and Sweetheart" will all bark at me. The kennel is now unloosed: all the pack—from the deep-mouthed bloodhound of South Carolina and Florida to the growling cur of Georgia—are baying at me. If I were to stop to throw stones at all the snarling puppies that yelp at my heels in South Carolina and elsewhere, I should have little time to do any thing else.

Your first falsehood, as gathered from a Knoxville writer, is that my subscription has so diminished of late that my office does not pay expenses. There are twelve newspapers in East Tennessee besides mine, and I have more paying subscribers than all of them put together. I have the largest list of any political paper in the State; and my list of yearly subscribers is now larger than it ever was before—increasing now at the rate of two hundred per week, and the rise of that. So much for my prospects of starving out.

2. But my town and county have cast a majority of their votes for Secession, and my State was to have done so! Well, sir, on Saturday last [February 9] our election was held, and a full vote was had all over the State—the issue being Union or Disunion. In my town, out of a vote of 960 the Secession ticket received 113, and in the remainder of the county the Secession ticket received about 100 votes, leaving the Union majority in the county and town *upwards of three thousand!* In the State

at large the Secession ticket is so badly beaten as to be absolutely disgraced. It has been "routed, horse, foot, and dragoon," the Secessionists having elected only about *half a dozen* members to the State Convention!

3. As to my thirst for office, I simply have to say that I never declared myself for office in my life. I have been frequently urged to run, but declined. There is but one office within the gift of my State that I would accept, and that is the office of *Governor*; and I am not sure that I will not run for this. I would like to fill that office for two years, in order to meet the issues that will be raised by the seceding States and traitors of the South; and, further, to take the State Bank and its numerous branches out of the hands of the Secessionists, who now have them in charge.

4. I am indebted to no stores in this or any other town, and I would not give the Republic of South Carolina twenty-five dollars to pay all my store-debts in this world. I have never been refused credit in any store here, and I am of the opinion that there is not a store in this city but would be willing to credit me for more than they can induce me to purchase.

5. The assertion that my partisan friends refuse to endorse any thing I say is simply an unmitigated falsehood. The Secession candidates have never made such an issue, and, if they were to, they would be promptly met by my "partisan friends." As it regards the sending to other sections of the State for papers by the common people of my county, it is simply a lie. I have, to-day, a larger list of subscribers in this county than any paper ever had, published in or out of the county. The "common people" are with me in sentiment, and the recent election shows that in this large county, voting something under four thousand votes, only two hundred and thirty-eight of them refused to endorse my "doctrines" at the ballot-box.

6. The last of your six propositions is the only one that contains a *squinting* towards the truth, and it, as a whole, is basely false. There are a few of the members of the Methodist Church in this city, Democrats and Secessionists, who do not interchange civilities with me, and have, for aught I know to the contrary, no sort of respect for me. If these entertain more profound contempt for me than I do for them, they are

truly objects of pity. And if the great body of the "common people," in the town and county, have no more respect for me and my "doctrines" than they have for these Methodist brethren of mine, I would leave the country, and settle where I could find persons agreeing with me in "doctrines." Upon these persons, wanting in respect for me as they are, I have no disposition to make war. The alarming and wasteful disease of *Disunion* is now raging among them and *prostrating* its victims. If their symptoms grow worse, and the disease continue to spread, I may, through compassion, convert the basement of my office into a *hospital* for the afflicted! Already their elongated faces evince to the passers-by that they have passed the Rubicon!

In conclusion, allow me to inform you, Mr. Cinclair, that in Tennessee the heresy of Secession, sick with contradiction and crazed with a superabundance of inconsistency, is flying to falsehood as a remedy, and expiring from the venom of its own fangs. The night of TREASON has passed away in Tennessee; the purple morn of PATRIOTISM has dawned. Already do the tints of truth appear, while the gloomy mists rising from the swamps of a polluted Southern Confederacy fade in the distance, and sink below the horizon to rise no more! A cloudless day is breaking around us in Tennessee; emerging from the ocean of the UNION, the sun of American liberty is rising along the whole line of the border States, refulgent in light, brilliant with patriotism, and resplendent in glory! The hallowed name of the AMERICAN UNION, more fragrant than the spicy gales of Arabia, more balmy than Gilead's air, thrills the bosom of the patriot, where despair once revelled, and whispers *good tidings for all lovers of the Union*! Trophies of victory, in smiles and peace, deck the brows of those who were once saddened with doubt and uncertainty and sunk with sorrows to the depth of hell.

Parent of good, these are thy works! Thou art the great mover in the minds of deluded and distracted men, and wilt turn them "as the rivers are turned," until they shall see thy glory, bask in the sunshine of our national prosperity, and drink living waters at the wells of American salvation!

Finally, sir, when you put forth your batch of villainous falsehoods, through the *brawling Jacobin journals* of a demoralized Southern Confederacy, have the *candor* and *charity* to accompany them with this reply, and I will remain the defiant opponent of a wilful and despicable South Carolina rascal!

W. G. Brownlow

Announcement to the People of Tennessee, March 23, 1861

Fellow Citizens:

As there seems to be a tardiness on the part of aspiring men in the State to declare themselves candidates for the office of Governor at the ensuing August election, and as the people seem a little slow in moving in that direction, I take this method of informing you that I am a candidate for the office. I come before you upon my own responsibility, without solicitations from, or consultations with, the Politicians of the State. To them I do not look for "aid and comfort," as they are aware that they can never control me, if in office, or use me to promote the objects of selfish cliques or factions. I look to the unbought and unterrified People of the State to elect me, and as I purpose, if elected, to serve them and their interests only, I desire to be elected by their suffrages and influence. I have confidence in the real people of the State, and will bow to their decision as expressed through the ballot-box, without one word of complaint though that decision may be against me. I should despise myself if I could resort to any of the tricks of the demagogue to secure the votes of the honest yeomanry of the country—such as arraying the poor against the rich, boasting of my humble origin, claiming my right to be elected upon sectional grounds or upon local issues, advocating a reduction of the salaries of public officers, and otherwise appealing to the passions and prejudices of the people. But I may be allowed to say that I have no wealth to make me prominent among the "upper tens." I have no long train of influential relatives to urge my claims. Losing my parents when a small boy, and being left without means, I went to the trade of the *house-carpenter*, and, after acquiring a knowledge of the "profession," I worked for wages long enough to enable me to acquire an "old field-school English education," adding to my store of knowledge in after-years as best I could. Whilst I do not think I ought to be supported *because of these things*, I do not think that any class of my fellow-countrymen ought to vote against me on this account. I ask for the votes of the people of Tennessee for the high and responsible office of Governor, only on account of the *political principles* I claim to represent. These I will, in brief, lay before the public, concealing nothing that ought to be made known.

1. It may be proper for me, as briefly as possible, to point out the circumstances which existed when this Confederacy and Constitution were formed. There exists now no question, political or otherwise, that did not then exist; and hence what is alleged to be the cause of the present attempt at the dissolution of this Government is a sheer fabrication, founded upon political chicanery, despotism, folly, and personal ambition. When the Constitution of the United States was formed, and was sought to be ratified by the various States which then composed the colonies, afterwards called the United States of America, there existed precisely the same elements, and many more subjects of diverse opinion and controversy than now. These were, first, the despotism and tyranny of monarchical power, that refused to grant to the colonies their just rights, for which in 1776 these united colonies waged successful war against Great Britain. *Afterwards*, for the purpose of mutual protection against invasion, it was deemed advisable to form a Confederacy—that Confederacy to represent the *people* of the United States, and not, as is contended by Secessionists, the "Sovereign States of America." Our fathers, declaring their independence, threw off the oppression of the mother-country, and summed up their grievances as "Taxation Without Representation." We have again in our midst a *bogus* form of Government, forced upon the Cotton States by an organized band of revolutionists, whose very foundation is that of "taxation without representation."

2. In consequence of diversity of climate, interests, and population, it was necessary to have certain *sectional* lines. Those lines already existed to a certain extent; and therefore it was deemed advisable to retain them, to prevent confusion. But the Constitution was formed by the *people* to govern the *people*, and no single individual State was called upon, as a separate "sovereignty," to sign or ratify that Constitution, but the representatives of each State were called upon to ratify it

for the *people* of that State. Therefore it was that not in one, nor two, but many years of debate and controversy, as well as of amendments and substitutes, the Constitution was adopted and ratified by all the States of the then existing Union. No State, therefore, belonging to the compact, has a right to withdraw without *consulting* with the other members. Originally, the States coming in were obliged to consult their *sectional* interests; they were obliged to call in question the various political and social differences then existing; they were obliged to question peculiar rights, to touch upon delicate points that then, more than now, bore upon the interests, welfare, and prosperity of the Union. And all who are at all acquainted with the history of our Government know that the hobby then is the bone of contention now among politicians; that it constituted not a sectional or State policy, strictly speaking, but a NATIONAL FACT; that it was considered and reconsidered; that concession after concession, plan after plan, was sought for, in order to prevent any future difficulty upon this eternal question of African slavery. I take occasion to assert that the question has not changed its relation to the General Government since then, and that, while the people of the North, then possessing slavery, desired that it should be abolished, the South clearly and distinctly understood that it was to continue here. Therefore it was made a constitutional fact that slavery should exist in every State of the Union, if the *people* of each State should so decide; and if the people of one or more States decided that it was against their interests to hold slaves, slavery should be abolished—where not abolished, it should be protected and sustained under the Constitution. And it is known to every political historian that the patriots who formed the Constitution agreed in *secret session*, deliberating upon the welfare of the nation, that it was important to prevent any future disquiet or discussion upon the Slavery question, and that therefore it should be left as a matter of purely *sectional* interest, with which the General Government has nothing to do and for which it would not be responsible, save that it would protect the interests of all the States choosing to adhere to slavery.[13]

13. Brownlow omitted here a passage from his original announcement. It strongly condemned the so-called personal liberty laws passed by northern states to hinder slaveowners trying to retrieve slaves who had escaped to the North. It is to these laws

3. It was the sworn duty of James Buchanan to suppress this rebellion when it first appeared, and before it grew up into its present gigantic proportions. Instead of doing his duty, he actually sat in converse with the TRAITORS engaged in the TREASON, received them into his presence, held counsel with them, and treated them with deference, instead of issuing an order for their arrest. He even consulted his Attorney-General as to the constitutionality of what was going on. An American President asks if it is constitutional to suppress rebellion or treason—if it is constitutional to hang a traitor—when the very spirit as well as the letter of the Constitution is death to all treason! What I advocate is this: that our Government execute its laws. If a million of lives are sacrificed, the other twenty-nine millions will have the benefits of freedom. And to the people of Tennessee I would say, in the name of your Constitution, in the name of your country, in the name of your forefathers, in the name of your children, your honors, your free institutions, I conjure you, give no ear to that insidious voice of treason which says peaceable secession will put an end to our troubles. In the same breath, I would say to the people of the North, repeal those acts which are wrong and unconstitutional. The nation requires it; your Government requires it; children unborn, who are to represent you in the future, urge it; all your future welfare and glory among men require it; and the dictates of your holy religion require it.

4. I stand where I did in the late Presidential contest, and never can stand anywhere else; that is to say, upon the platform of the "UNION, THE CONSTITUTION, AND THE ENFORCEMENT OF THE LAWS." I do not believe that the election of Lincoln affords any sort of pretext for dissolving this Union; I deny the right of secession; I regard the States that have gone out of the Union as guilty of TREASON; and I view the leaders of the Secession party as TRAITORS. If elected Governor, I would refuse to convene the Legislature or take any step that would advance the cause of Secession, and treat them as men guilty of breaches of good faith and common honesty.[14]

---

that Brownlow alludes (in considerably milder terms) at the end of the following paragraph.

14. The Parson here omitted another passage, in which he bitterly denounced the radical northern abolitionists, who, he said, were as guilty as the secessionists of seeking the dissolution of the Union.

5. I endorse the Inaugural Address of Lincoln, and I commend it for its temperance and conservatism and for its firm nationality of sentiment. From it I infer that we shall have no war *unless* it be forced upon the country by the Seceding States. If Lincoln should attempt to inaugurate oppressive and unconstitutional measures, and Congress shall sanction or adopt these measures, either in reference to the Slavery question or any other subject, we of the South should await the decision of the Supreme Court, and if the Executive, Legislative, and Judicial departments of the Government all sanction such iniquitous measures and unite in attempts to carry them out, then, and in that case, I would advocate resistance "at all hazards and to the last extremity." But, until this is apparent, it is the duty of this patriotic State to stand firm, and not entangle herself with the extremes of either the North or South, and to act upon the sound maxim that *Disunion* is not a remedy for any wrongs whatever.

6. The leaders in this movement to dissolve this Union, the great citadel of our liberties, and the depository of the hopes of the human race, will go down to their graves without any halo of glory surrounding their brows, while on their heads will be gathered the hissing curses of all generations, horrible as the forked-tongued snakes of Medusa. Their ghosts will stand on the highest and blackest eminence of infamy, the detestation of mankind. Having met a traitor's death, they will each and all fill a traitor's grave, over which there will be no requiem but the groans of the oppressed and the execrations of the good. Their monuments will be of human bones upon foundations slippery with human blood. However high may have been their elevation in office, their fall will be like that of Lucifer. And whilst from their bad eminence they shall turn from beholding the glories of that Constitution and Union against which they rebelled in the year of grace 1861, to survey the barren waste, the boundless and bottomless pits, of Secession, they will exclaim, like Lucifer, their "illustrious predecessor"—

> Farewell, happy fields! where joy forever dwells!
> Hail, horrors! hail, infernal world! and thou,
> Profoundest hell! receive thy new possessor!

7. I claim to have had no lot or part in bringing upon the country the terrible crisis that is now upon us. The late Chief Magistrate, James

Buchanan, was inaugurated into office under auspices of general peace and prosperity—strong in the confidence of a mighty, united, and triumphant Democracy. Possessed of every aid and inducement to an honest, a patriotic, a brilliant, and a vigorous and successful administration of the Government, he has retired from power amid general execration and disgrace, carrying into his retirement the official brand of public condemnation upon his forehead, and leaving to history, as the only trophies of his administration, the national treasury depleted, the country loaded with an incubus of debt, that great national and conservative party, to whose generous and confiding suffrages he owes all his fortunes, demoralized and dismembered, the perpetuity of the republic a doubtful and an appalling problem, and his own name a byword of infamy and derision throughout the civilized world. And in this State the men are in power, wielding its patronage, who travelled all over the State defending this corrupt Administration after the proof of its infamy was before the world, both clear and unquestionable.

The policy of the new Administration is not yet fully developed. Taking the nomination of that great and good man, Mr. Crittenden, to the Supreme Court as an example, it has manifested thus far only conservative tendencies, and it has afforded proof that it does not seek to abolitionize the Judiciary.[15] It would be more reasonable, more prudent, and infinitely safer for the people of the South patiently to await the developments of the policy of the new Administration, than to fly from the ills they have to others that they know not of, and which are already creating so much discontent in the new Confederacy. That I may be fully understood, I repeat that I am for the Union as it came to us from our fathers—the most glorious legacy of modern times. I believe it ought to be preserved. It should be maintained by *peaceable* means—and this can be done; but if the property [i.e., forts] belonging to the General Government and now in its possession, and costing the common people of all the States millions of dollars, cannot be held except by force and against the assaults of the Rebels going out of the Union, I say, boldly, let the gates of the temple of Janus open; let a na-

15. The rumor that President Lincoln intended to appoint prominent Kentucky Unionist John J. Crittenden to the Supreme Court was widespread at this time but proved to be untrue.

tional blow be given which will resound—like the shouts of Michael's host hurling treason over the ramparts of heaven—through all the avenues of unrecorded time.

8. I protest against a surrender of the navigation of the Mississippi River, and would not, if elected to the office of Governor, agree to relinquish the right Tennessee has to the free navigation of that great "inland sea," if even the General Government should basely surrender its rights and the rights of the several Western and Northwestern States. Nor am I willing to recognize the act of Secession on the part of Florida, Louisiana, and Texas in any other light than that of *dishonesty* and *treason*, meriting the scorn and contempt of the civilized world. I say this because of the vast amount of money paid by our Government, to say nothing of the sacrifice of human life, for the exclusive benefit of these three States [i.e., expenses incurred in purchasing and securing control over the three territories]. . . .

Ought these three rebellious States to be tolerated in their mad schemes of plunder and treason, after costing the people of the other States *six hundred and eighteen millions of dollars?* I say, No; and, as the Executive of this State, I could never do an act that would in the remotest degree tolerate this wholesale robbery.

9. The President of the new Confederacy [Jefferson Davis] has confined his Cabinet appointments to the old Democratic party—appointing none but Breckinridge Disunionists, although the Bell and Douglas men were a majority in some of their States. The provisional Government is, therefore, a revival of corrupt Southern Democracy, and is a lawless mob banded together for the purpose of perpetuating that exploded, hateful, and God-forsaken organization. It is not *a government of the people*, and it will not long be tolerated by the people. The people, *who ought to be the source of power*, have been refused the privilege of passing upon any one of their ordinances of Secession, and now they are to be refused the privilege of passing upon their Constitution. I would sooner go into the worst form of European monarchy than into this *bogus* Confederacy. And if elected Governor of this State, I will oppose, to the bitter end, any fellowship with such Confederacy by the State of Tennessee.

10. I take the ground steadfastly to support the General Government in the exercise of every constitutional power, to enforce the exe-

cution of the Federal laws, and to sustain in all their integrity the Constitution and the Union. In other words, I do not propose to sit quietly by and peacefully surrender our country, ourselves, our children, our peace and happiness, to the wicked schemes of *treason.* We hear much said about "coercing" a State, and about the tramp of hostile armies to conquer and subdue a State Government. Coercion of a State is an adroit form of expression, coined in the school of Secession to give dignity to treason. The American Constitution nowhere contemplates such a thing as war upon a State, either by the General Government or by a foreign Power. If a foreign nation attack or invade any State of the Union, it is not, in the theory of the Constitution or of international law, an act of war upon the State, but upon our General Government. Nor does the Constitution, operating as it does only upon individuals, recognize such a thing as war against the Government by a State, or an association of States. It treats resistance to its authority as *rebellion*, and those who join in such resistance as a Mob; and when any number of its own citizens band together for treasonable purposes, and levy war upon the General Government, it holds them individually responsible, and hangs them as traitors to this country. The founders of the Government avowed that it afforded the needful physical means to execute its powers. History gives us memorable examples of the use of those means for their purpose.

I repeat that the word "coercion" is one in very common use in these days, and it is very offensive to all advocates of Disunion. Like many other *catch*-words, it serves a purpose. Any thing looking to the enforcement of the laws, or the preservation of the public property in seceded States, or States about to secede, is called *coercion*, and the honest and confiding people are warned against it as a fearful despotism! This *trick*, like every thing else, will, in some quarters, serve its purpose. I deny the right of any State or number of States to secede, and I insist upon it that the seceded States, one and all, are *constitutionally* as much in the Union as they were six months ago. While laws exist in reference to them, it is the duty of the Government to enforce them. If this cannot or ought not to be done, why, let them be repealed. This the public good and the national honor alike require. A State cannot be *coerced*, but *individuals* in it can, and *ought* to be, who violate the laws and plot treason.

And although I look upon the withdrawal of the troops from Fort
Sumter as an act of humiliation on the part of the Government, I approve the act, under all the circumstances which surround us, and I
consider that it removes all danger of civil war.[16] It is a master-stroke
of policy, and by it the rabid Disunionists have been disarmed, and deprived of all their thunder—leaving them nothing to cavil at, nothing
to attack, nothing over which they can pretend to get in a passion.
While this evacuation of Fort Sumter removes all danger of immediate
collision, it will disabuse the minds of deluded Southerners as to the alleged aggressive character of the Administration, and will do more
than all that has been proposed towards suppressing Disunion, and re-
calling the masses of our countrymen in the South to their sober senses,
and to their rightful allegiance to the Union and the Constitution, and
the Stars and Stripes by which they are represented. Every man,
woman, and child, in every locality of our once happy land, should de-
voutly labor for the peaceful solution of our unfortunate political dif-
ficulties. With peace, we may anticipate happiness and plenty; with
war, crime, poverty, wretchedness, weeping, lamentation, and sorrow
all over the land.

11. As it regards State policy, I am the advocate of establishing a
branch of the penitentiary in the Western District, and another in East
Tennessee. The cost of building to the State would be saved in twenty-
five years in the single item of conveying the convicts to prison. Besides
this, it would open up a cash-market to the citizens in each end of the
State for provisions to sustain, and raw material to keep, the convicts
employed in manufacturing—such as lumber, marble, iron, leather,
&c. This would furnish employment, and cash wages, to quite a number of mechanics in each division of our State; and, as there are several
salaried offices in each, it would distribute the patronage of the State
in her three natural divisions.

12. The Governor has the control of a heavy patronage in the railroads and banks of the State; and this is all now in the hands of Secessionists, who must be swept from office, or the public interests will suf-

16. It was widely believed that Lincoln had decided to evacuate Fort Sumter to
avoid a military showdown with the Confederacy. This rumor was, of course, false.

fer, and the State treasury will bleed at every pore, as it has been doing in several of the banks! It would be my duty, if elected, to turn these men out; and I would take the greatest pleasure in removing them. Neither the bank of the State, nor any of its *dozen* branches, are under the control of farmers, mechanics, and laboring-men; but they are, each and all, controlled by political partisan leaders, county-court lawyers, and street-loafers. If I am elected, the iniquitous reign of these pampered bank-officers and recipients of bank-favors is at an end! . . .

In most of these branch banks, men have been refused discounts, when they have presented well-endorsed paper, on account of their politics, although the State has recently declared against the politics of these same bank-officers by a majority of SEVENTY THOUSAND VOTES! Thus the banks of the people are used against their owners by a mere faction who have them in charge. The Secessionists also have the arms of the State in their possession, distributed by the present Governor [Isham Harris].

The Disunionists of Tennessee ought to, and I suppose will, long remember the ever-memorable 9th of February, 1861. On that day the freemen of the State were called upon to vote for and against a Convention, for and against Disunion. The vote stood thus, in eighty-one counties in the State:

No Convention	69,675
Convention	57,798
Majority against Convention	11,877

This was a decided vote against the first step of the Disunionists to drag Tennessee into a detestable Confederacy, and out from under the protection of the Stars and Stripes. But when the people came to elect delegates, the Disunionists received a majority in only *four* counties, the vote footing up thus:

Union	88,803
Disunion	24,749

Thus the Union party received a majority, after a thorough canvass, of 64,054 in the State, with six other counties to hear from, which will increase the majority to 70,000. Never was such a victory achieved in any State! Ought a *faction*, therefore, representing twenty-five thousand out of one hundred and twenty thousand votes polled, to hold the offices of the State and control her patronage, when that faction is seeking to destroy the Government? I say, most emphatically, No! And if the people think proper to elect me, I will see that they cease to control the patronage of the State.

13. I am frank to confess that I desire the position on account of its honor, and as a means of rebuking my numerous Southern calumniators, who are unrelenting in their abusive war upon me because of my Union sentiments and of my opposition to their treason. I shall, of course, if elected, hope to serve the interests of the people of the whole State, irrespective of parties. But, not being rich, I would like to fill the office for two years, for the sake of the THREE THOUSAND DOLLARS PER ANNUM. Candor requires these avowals.

14. If voted for, and elected, it must be done without my canvassing the State, or speaking to the people otherwise than through a circular. Though my general health is good, and constantly improving, I have suffered for two years past from *bronchitis*, or a disease of the throat, rendering it impossible for me to speak loud enough to be heard ten steps. Now that I am able to speak in moderation for one hour, I dare not do this more than once in a week; and I would fear to do even this many weeks in succession. The people of the State know me, and they know my politics. I have edited a WHIG paper in East Tennessee for the last twenty-two years. I still edit that paper, and it circulates in every county in the State, and there can really be no necessity for my canvassing.

The demand made upon the standard-bearer in this State, for the last quarter of a century, of all parties, to canvass the whole State, at an outlay of several hundred dollars, and an amount of labor and fatigue ruinous to the constitution, has caused many of our best men to decline the position of candidate for Governor, and to remain in private life. The present is a suitable time to abandon the practice of stumping the State; and I propose to lead the way in this *reform*. If any candidate, of any party, running in opposition to me, shall think proper to arraign me upon *personalities*, and to *denounce* me in my absence, and attribute my declining to canvass the State to *cowardice*, I will make one appointment to meet him at some prominent point, and, from the same stand, meet his assaults with *personalities* and *denunciations*, publish my speech to the world, distribute it over the State, and let the people settle the dispute as to personal courage.

15. If the real people, who constitute the great Union party in the State, shall prefer some other candidate to me, and shall make that fact known by a distinct and legitimate expression of their will, uninfluenced by leaders and wire-workers, I will not be the man to disturb the harmony of the Union organization: I will at once fall into line, and enter most heartily into the support of their choice—*provided,* always, that the standard-bearer avows *substantially* the doctrines I have herein enunciated. A time-serving man, and a trimmer, cannot get my support, though he run as the representative of the principles of the great Union party and succeed in obtaining the nomination by a State Convention. The progressive exigencies of our country imperatively demand of a man aspiring to an office of such honor and trust, that he *show his hand in unmistakable terms!*

In this I do not mean to dictate to the party or their candidate their political creed, or to set up my standard as one of political perfection. I simply mean to say that a candidate falling short in the political articles of faith I enunciate cannot receive my vote; though, if nominated, I will not make war upon him, or give him any factious opposition. And this circular, in lieu of the hastily-sketched address I put forth last week, is the PLATFORM upon which I propose to run this race; and if I have not clearly defined my position, it is because I am not capable of expressing my opinions.

16. From the press of the State I ask that courtesy and consideration which it is accustomed to extend to new candidates for popular favor—that of copying this circular entire; each paper reserving to itself the universally conceded right to condemn each and every part. Such papers as do not think proper to yield so much of their space to my service will do me the simple act of justice not to give garbled extracts and in that way misrepresent my sentiments.

I have the honor to be,
Very respectfully, &c.,

W. G. BROWNLOW

CORRESPONDENCE, 1861

Albany, N.Y., May 8, 1861

W. G. BROWNLOW, Esq.:

I send you by mail the Albany *Evening Journal*, containing Hon. Benj. Nott's speech on the crisis. Judge Nott is a life-long Democrat, of the Hard-Shell school, and an avowed advocate of the Dred Scott decision.[17]

I read your paper with great interest, and your course is the subject of conversation in every circle North, meeting the approval of all parties, for all parties here are for the Union. We understand you to be a pro-Slavery man, but for the Union, opposed to Secession—not even regarding the election of Lincoln as any just cause for dissolving the Union. Can't you give us a leading editorial on these points, and at the same time state the position of the Union men in the border Slave States in the event the Administration were to interfere in any way with the institution of slavery?

The masses of the Northern people have no feelings but the most friendly towards their brethren of the South, and are ready to concede to them all their rights. They are even for returning to them their slaves who have escaped, as the law requires. This Administration would protect Southern rights, and if it would not of choice, the public would require it to be done. And, in saying this, I assure you I am no Lincoln man. But this you very well know.

Hoping that you may be sustained, and live to see the Stars and Stripes float on every hill-top, and in every valley, from the St. Lawrence to the Rio Grande, I remain, very truly,

L. M. E.

Knoxville, May 14, 1861

To L. M. E.:

I have your letter of the 8th, and also the *Evening Journal*. I have perused the speech of Judge Nott: it is able, conservative, and eminently

17. In the Dred Scott case of 1857, the U.S Supreme Court declared Congress had no power to bar slavery from a territory. Though widely hailed in the South, the decision angered all but the most conservative northerners.

patriotic. Had you more Notts in the North, and fewer Slavery agitators, and had we fewer Rhetts,[18] Yanceys, and Davises, in the South, none of these troubles would now be upon the country.

You correctly interpret the Union men of the border Slave States when you pronounce them "pro-Slavery men." I think I correctly represent them in my paper, as I shall do in this brief epistle, except, perhaps, that I am more *ultra* than most of them. I am a native of Virginia, and so were my parents before me, and, together with a numerous train of relatives, they were and are slave-holders. For thirty years I have lived in Tennessee, and my wife and children are native Tennesseans. My native State did more to form the old Confederacy and to form the Constitution of the United States than any other State; her soil is now the resting-place of the honored dead, the most ultra old Unionists dead or alive—Washington, Jefferson, Madison, Monroe, Marshall, Henry, and a host of others. I am sorry to have to record that it has, in the mysterious providence of God, been reserved to Virginia to do more towards overthrowing the Confederacy and the Constitution than any other State, South Carolina not even excepted. It took the Virginia [Secession] Convention of 1861 to overthrow her State Government—changing her organic political *status* contrary to the expressed direction of her people at the ballot-box when they elected the men who perpetrated the deed! Virginia, I am sorry to say, if I may be allowed to use an humble illustration, is like a *hill of potatoes*—the best part under ground: the part above ground reminds me but of *vines*. When citizens of other States are called upon to name their great statesmen, they point to *living men*. Make the call upon Virginians, and they ask you out into *a graveyard*, when they will point you to the tomb of Washington, the monument erected over Madison, or the grave of Jefferson!

I am a pro-Slavery man, and so are the Union men generally of the border Slave States. I have long since made up my mind upon the Slavery question, but not without studying it thoroughly. The result of my investigation is, that there is not a single passage in the New Testament, nor a single act in the records of the Church, during her early

18. Robert Barnwell Rhett of South Carolina was a prominent southern "fire-eater."

history even for centuries, containing any direct, professed, or *intended* censure of slavery. Christ and the apostles found the institution existing under the authority and sanction of law; and in their labors among the people, unlike *ultra* Abolitionists, *masters* and *slaves* bowed at the same altars, and were taken into the same Church, communing together around the same table—the Saviour and his apostles exhorting *owners* to treat *slaves* as became the gospel, and slaves to obedience and honesty, that their religious profession might not be evil spoken of.

The original Church of Christ not only admitted the lawfulness of slavery, but in various ways, by her teachings and discipline, expressed her *approbation* of it, enforcing the observance of "Fugitive Slave Laws" which had been enacted by the State. God intended the relation of master and slave to exist, both *in* and *out* of his Church. Hence, when Christ and his apostles found slavery *incorporated with every department of society*, they went to work and adopted rules for the government of the Church providing alike for the *rights* of slave-holders and the *wants* of slaves. Slavery in the days of the apostles had so penetrated society, and was so intimately interwoven with it, that a religion *preaching freedom to the slaves* would have arrayed against it the civil authorities, armed against it the whole power of the State, and destroyed the usefulness of its preachers.

Finally, I hold—and thirty years of observation and experience among slave-holders in the South have convinced me that I am not mistaken—that all the finer feelings of humanity may be cherished in the bosoms of slave-owners; that there are thousands of devout slave-owners and slaves in the South who are acceptable to God, through Christ. And, however much the bonds of the slaves of the South may provoke the wrath of the ultra Abolitionists of the North, the Redeemer of the world smiles alike upon the devout master and the pious slave!

Now, sir, allow me further to say that the Union men of the border Slave States are loyal to their Government, and do not regard the election of Lincoln as any just cause for dissolving this Union. We believe that slavery had very little to do with inaugurating armed secession, which commenced at Charleston, to overthrow the United States Government: it was the loss of the offices, power, and patronage of the Government by corrupt politicians and bad men in the South, who had long controlled the Government. Believing this, as we honestly do, we can never, like Mexico, inaugurate political conflicts and anarchy by armed secession. We can never agree to assist in the inauguration of a Government of conventions by armed secession—which Government, in the case of England and her Rump Parliament, resulted in the Protectorate of Cromwell, and in France, in the military despotism of Bonaparte, and in both cases resulted in anarchy, as it is bound to do in this country if not put down by the power of the Government.

Whilst I say this, let me say, in all candor, that if we were once convinced in the border Slave States that the Administration at Washington, and the people of the North who are backing up the Administration with men and money, contemplated the *subjugation* of the South or the *abolishing* of slavery, there would not be a Union man among us in twenty-four hours. Come what might, sink or swim, survive or perish, we would fight you to the death, and we would unite our fortunes and destinies with even these demoralized seceded States, for whose leaders and laws we have no sort of respect. But we have not believed, nor do we yet believe, that the Administration has such purposes in view. Demagogues and designing men charge it here, and by this means enlist thousands under their banner who, otherwise, would never support their wicked schemes of Secession. We Union men believe that the blow was struck upon Fort Sumter to induce Virginia to go out, and to create sympathy elsewhere, and that the Administration at Washington is seeking to repossess its forts and property and to preserve its existence; and, as long as we believe this, we are for the Union and the Administration. I, of course, speak for Union men in the general. We are sustained in this by the Mobile *Advertiser*, which glories in the fact that the seven Confederated States "*struck the first blow in the conflict*," and "*threw down the glove of mortal combat to their powerful foe.*" The Mobile organ of Secession adds, "It was plucky in the seven Confederates: it was more—it was sublimely courageous and patriotic."

Allow me to say that the curse of the country has been that, for years, north of Mason & Dixon's line, you have kept pulpits open to the abuse of Southern slavery and of the Southern people.[19]

In like manner, the clergy of the South—without distinction of sects—men of talents, learning, and influence—have raised the howl of Secession, and it falls like an Indian war-cry upon our citizens from their prostituted pulpits every Sabbath. Many of them go so far as to petition their God, in their public prayers, to *blast* the people of the North! I have no idea that a God of peace will answer any such blasphemous supplications; but it shows the spirit of these minions of anarchy, who have sworn allegiance to the kingdom of Davis, and have been released from any further obligations to the kingdom of Jesus—at least during the war! Some of our clergy are officers in volunteer companies, with swords hung to their sides, and stripes on their pants. Others, having an eye to the loaves and fishes, are anxious to serve as chaplains.

We are in the midst of a reign of terror in Tennessee, and where it will end, and in what, I am not able to conjecture. We vote for or against the Ordinance of Secession on the 8th of June; and, although there is a majority of the voters of the State utterly and irreconcilably opposed to Secession, I can't promise you that it will not carry.[20] Fraud and force, and all the other appliances of Secessionism, will be brought to bear in carrying the State out of the Union. When overpowered and voted down, we shall be forced to submit. When I surrender, it will be because I can no longer help myself; but it shall be under protest, claiming the right, as a Union man, to curse this whole movement in

19. Brownlow deleted the remainder of this paragraph as it originally appeared in the *Whig*. The banished passage contained a severe denunciation of the northern clergy, who, he claimed, had deluded and inflamed the people of the North.

20. Soon after the bombardment of Fort Sumter, Governor Harris called the legislature into special session. On May 6 it passed a Declaration of Independence taking Tennessee out of the Union, stipulating, however, that the legislation would not take effect unless approved by the voters in a June 8 referendum. Without waiting for the referendum, Tennessee secessionists by the thousands began enlisting to fight the Yankees, while Governor Harris took steps to align the state with the Confederacy; he even allowed Confederate troops from other states to be posted in Tennessee. On June 8, Tennessee voters endorsed the state's secession by an overall margin of 68 to 32 percent. In East Tennessee, however, the vote was more than two to one against secession.

my heart of hearts! And, whether in or out of the Union, as long as I remember it was Washington who told us, "*The Constitution is sacredly obligatory upon all*"; and that it was Jackson who told us, "*The Union, it must be preserved*"—I shall offer this prayer upon the altar of my country: Mania to the brain of him who would conceive, and palsy to the arm of him who would perpetrate, the dissolution of the Union!

And, whether my humble voice is hushed in death, or my press is muzzled by foul legislation, I beg you, and all into whose hands this letter may fall, to credit no Secession falsehood which may represent me as having changed.

W. G. BROWNLOW

EDITORIAL, MAY 25, 1861

It is known to this community and to the people of this county that I have had the Stars and Stripes, in the character of a small flag, floating over my dwelling, in East Knoxville, since February. This flag has become very offensive to certain leaders of the Secession party in this town, and to certain would-be leaders, and the more so as it is about the only one of the kind floating in the city. Squads of troops, from three to twenty, have come over to my house, within the last several days, cursing the flag in front of my house, and threatening to take it down, greatly to the annoyance of my wife and children. No attack has been made upon it, and consequently we have had no difficulty. It is due to the Tennessee troops to say that they have never made any such demonstrations. Other troops from the Southern States, passing on to Virginia, have been induced to do so, by certain cowardly, sneaking, white-livered scoundrels, residing here, who have not the *melt* to undertake what they urge strangers to do. One of the Louisiana squads proclaimed in front of my house, on Thursday, that they were told to take it down by citizens of Knoxville.

Now, I wish to say a few things to the public in connection with this subject. This flag is private property, upon a private dwelling, in a State that has *never voted herself out of the Union* or into the Southern Confederacy, and is therefore lawfully and constitutionally under these same Stars and Stripes I have floating over my house. Until the State, by her citizens, through the ballot-box, changes her Federal relations, her citizens have a right to fling this banner to the breeze. Those who are in rebellion against the Government represented by the Stars and Stripes have up the Rebel flag, and it is a high piece of work to deny loyal citizens of the Union the privilege of displaying their colors!

But there is one other feature of this tyranny and of these mobocratic assaults I wish to lay before the people, irrespective of parties. There are but a few of the leaders of this Secession movement in Knoxville— less than half a dozen—for whom I entertain any sort of respect, or whose good opinions I esteem. With one of these I had a free and full conversation, more than two weeks ago, in regard to this whole question. I told him that we Union men would make the best fight we could at the ballot-box, on the 8th of June, to keep the State in the Union; but that if we were overpowered, and a majority of the people of the State should say in this constitutional way that she must secede, we should have to come down, and bring our flags with us, bowing to the will of the majority with the best grace we could. I made the same statement to the colonel who got up a regiment here, and to one of his subordinate officers. I made the same statement to the president of the railroad, and I have repeatedly made the same statement through my paper. The whole Secession party here know this to be the position and purpose of the Union party; but a portion of them seek to bring about personal conflicts, and to engage strangers, under the influence of whiskey, to do a dirty and villainous work they have the meanness to do, without the courage.

If these God-forsaken scoundrels and hell-deserving assassins want satisfaction out of me for what I have said about them—and it has been no little—they can find me on these streets every day of my life but Sunday. I am at all times prepared to give them satisfaction. I take back nothing I have ever said against the corrupt and unprincipled villains, but reiterate all, cast it in their dastardly faces, and hurl down their lying throats their own infamous calumnies.

Finally, the destroying of my small flag or of my town-property is a small matter. The carrying out of the State upon the mad wave of Secession is also a small matter, compared with the great Principle involved. Sink or swim, live or die, survive or perish, I am a Union man, and owe my allegiance to the Stars and Stripes of my country. Nor can I, in any possible contingency, have any respect for the Government of the Confederated States, originating as it did with, and being controlled by, the worst men in the South. And any man saying—whether of high or low degree—that I am an Abolitionist or a Black Republican, is a LIAR and a SCOUNDREL.

CORRESPONDENCE, 1861

Cedar Grove, Fla., June 15, 1861

DR. BROWNLOW:

As a freeman, you have a right to your opinions, in common with other men, but, sir, you have no right to defame those who are laboring to throw off the yoke of Northern oppression. I have ever been an admirer of yours, and of your principles; but permit me to tell you this morning that you are doing more injury to the Cotton States than any of the Greeleys or Webbs[21] of Yankeedom. I do not believe you to be an Abolitionist, as some do in this quarter. These being my honest opinions, I do not wish to read your paper longer. If there be any thing due me on my subscription, I wish it applied to the family of Jackson the martyr.[22]

Very truly, &c.,

R. M. SCARBOROUGH

Knoxville, June 25, 1861

MR. SCARBOROUGH:

I received your letter of the 15th only on yesterday, and I hasten to reply very briefly. Upon examination, I find thirty cents due you on my book, and I enclose you the amount in United States stamps, which

21. Horace Greeley, publisher of the New York *Tribune*, and James Watson Webb, publisher of the New York *Courier and Enquirer*, were influential spokesmen.

22. James T. Jackson was a secessionist hotelkeeper in Alexandria, Virginia. On May 24, 1861, Union troops occupied the town. One officer, Colonel Elmer Ellsworth, spotted a secession flag flying from Jackson's hotel, rushed inside, and tore the flag down. Jackson shot him to death, but was then likewise killed by a Union soldier. The incident was widely publicized, in part because Ellsworth was a well-known figure in the North and a friend of Lincoln.

you can transmit to "the family of Jackson the martyr," who can use them in their locality.

You are correct in supposing me free from the taint of Abolitionism. I have fought the agitators of the Slavery question at the North for the last two-and-twenty years, during which time I have edited a Whig paper in Tennessee. With my *Government*, and its *Constitution* and *laws*, I intend to stand or fall, having no regard to who may be President for the time being. This rebellion is utterly without cause. Nothing but force will put it down; and hence there never was a more necessary, just, and lawful war than this, to preserve a necessary, just, and noble Government against inexcusable, unnatural, and villainous rebellion. This rebellion, on the part of the South, originated in falsehood, fraud, and perjury, and the men who inaugurated it, and are now at its head, are as bad men as ever agitated the Slavery question in New England, or any who suffer the vengeance of eternal fire for having flagrantly violated God's law through a long and eventful life of wickedness! Knowing this, or rather believing it, as I honestly do, I can have no sympathy with the men in the South who have brought about this war and are urging it on. No mad-dog cry of the invasion of the sacred soil of the South by the Vandals of the North can blind my eyes to the *facts* in the case, or shift the responsibilities of its origin upon those who are fighting to preserve the Government. Men need not talk to me about the unnatural, fratricidal, and horrible war Lincoln is waging! Why is it unnatural? I think it the most natural thing in the world for a nation to fight for its Government against a vile rebellion which has never yet been able to allege an excuse. That any portion of the people should stand aloof from such a cause, is indeed unnatural, but that does not make the war unnatural.

That any people should rebel against so benign a Government, and make war upon it, is most unnatural. It is the greatest crime that could be committed against humanity, for it and its consequences include all other crimes. It was not the falsely-alleged Slavery question that excited the Cotton States to the *fatal* point, and brought about their acts of secession. It was because they lost the race for the Presidency, and with it the spoils and power of a Government they had been plundering and living off of for years. Hence, it was only when the Govern-

ment changed hands, and, in the legitimate exercise of its lawful powers, resorted to the only means that would preserve it and a vestige of
liberty to the American people, that the war became unnatural, fratricidal, and horrible to the advocates of a Southern Confederacy. Southern-Rights politicians and hypocritical clergymen may ejaculate that
their heads may be made water, and their eyes fountains of tears, that
they may weep day and night over the unnatural war of the best Government that has ever existed, against the most villainous rebellion that
history gives any account of, and they can never excite my sympathies
but in favor of the Government.

The Secessionists, for the purpose of hiding their traitorous course,
create a false issue before the people. They assert that the effort to preserve the Government is an attempt on the part of the North to crush
the South, and that a sectional fight is the real issue before the people.
This attempt to create a false issue is an acknowledgment on their part
that they dare not meet the true one. The effort to enforce the law is
not a fight against the South, but it is a fight against the traitors to the
General Government; and, whether they appear North or South, it is
the duty of the Government to crush the treason. When Southern traitors resist the laws of the land, they call all attempts on the part of the
Administration to enforce those laws, outrageous acts of oppression—
attempts to invade and subjugate the free and independent people of
fifteen sovereign States. Rebellion with this class of men is liberty,
whilst they denounce all attempts to execute the laws of the land as the
essence of despotism. To such subterfuges are Secessionists driven to
sustain the rebellious course they have entered upon under a Southern
Confederacy.

For daring to oppose Secession, the chivalry of my own section have
denounced me in unmeasured terms, and declared me less sane than
the inmates of Bedlam. And because I have refused to lavish volumes
of whimsical abuse upon the North for their defence of the National
Government, I have been pelted with a most horrible bombardment of
uncleanly epithets by the veracious chroniclers who control the pensioned press of the South. The complaint against me is, that my paper
has not teemed with bragging and fantastical lies about the origin of
this war, and the ability of one Southern soldier to whip five Yankees.

I have been even required by my Southern subscribers to declare, upon the receipt of the news of every engagement by scouting-parties, that the Yankees took to their heels, and that soon the Southern troops would have the Yankees harnessed tandem-fashion, and with their own hands conveying them back to their Southern plantations in a Broadway omnibus! I have been expected to state in every issue of my paper, that the mantle of Washington sits well on Jeff Davis! This would be a funny publication. The bow of Ulysses in the hands of a pigmy! The robes of the giant adorning Tom Thumb! The curls of a Hyperion on the brow of a Satyr! The Aurora Borealis of a cotton farm melting down the icy North! This would be to metamorphose a *minnow* into a WHALE!

I never look through telescopes made of cotton-stalks, and hence I never make these ridiculous discoveries. And I tell the misguided men of the South, who have been laboring to make a demi-god of Davis, to undeceive themselves, and look at men "as trees walking." Look at battles as they occur, and at chances as they are. The deception they are imposing upon the honest masses is only temporary. It will become more and more apparent, as their humbugged victims draw near to the sober realities of a war which must terminate fatally for the interests of the South.

I assure you, my dear sir, that I am honest in my convictions of right, and that in advocating my Government I am not looking to a reward in dollars and cents. Indeed, I am a loser by my course, as I knew I would be; but I feel tranquil under losses incurred in the manly defence of PRINCIPLES. I shall look on the progress of affairs with as much interest as any one man in the country. If the Federal Government prevails, it will prove that the Union was a nationality; if the Cotton States make good their independence, it will prove that the Union was a partnership during pleasure. In other words, if we have a Government, I want to know it; and this war will determine the issue.

I am, sir, very truly,

W. G. BROWNLOW

EDITORIAL, JUNE 29, 1861

Bryant Breeden, an old man, some sixty years of age, and a very respectable citizen of Sevier county, recently had a daughter to die in Illinois, leaving several helpless and unprotected children. Mr. Breeden determined to go after his grandchildren, and took *Memphis* on his way. There he fell into the hands of the Secessionists, whose great concern for the *safety* of the South and her *rights* led them to arrest him. Upon learning that he hailed from East Tennessee, and from the odious Union county of Sevier, they procured a *rope*, and led him around, threatening every moment to hang him. He had, therefore, to abandon his trip, and leave his poor little orphan grandchildren to the mercy of strangers in Illinois. He was a quiet man while in Memphis, as he is at home—disturbed no one—but, when interrogated, acknowledged himself to be a Union man from East Tennessee, and for this, and no other offence, was he thus treated. This is the *spirit* which everywhere actuates the self-constituted Secession Committees of Safety, and the leaders of those most intolerant and odious organizations. No wonder that freemen of East Tennessee, by thousands, have resolved not to go into this Southern Confederacy! No wonder that the Union men of the thirty counties of East Tennessee should desire to be cut loose from the rest of the State, and allowed to form a separate State.[23] To live in such a Confederacy, under the control of such men, actuated by such a spirit, is literally to live in hell!

Editorial, July 6, 1861

One day last week, the Southern mail brought us a small package, done up precisely like a newspaper, and about equal in size to one of our exchanges, with the usual endorsement, "Brownlow's Whig, Knoxville, Tennessee," and postpaid. Upon opening it, we found it to contain about half a yard of brown domestic [cloth], with an appearance resembling that of a cloth taken from some one afflicted with small-pox. We had it burned in the front yard of our printing-office, after handling it with tongs! This is the *spirit* of Secession—its mode of warfare, and its sense of honor. Clever men, heretofore high-

23. Earlier in June, 285 East Tennessee Unionists (including Brownlow) had convened in Greeneville and passed resolutions condemning secession. They also sent a petition to Nashville, requesting that the legislature grant separate statehood to East Tennessee. The legislature rejected it.

minded, will not be long in their ranks until they will openly justify even this mode of warfare against Union men.

This attempt at our death, by the planting of a masked battery manned by the iniquitous spirit of Secession, entitles the cowardly villain who did it, to the honor of being picketed in the deepest gorge leading to hell! Not only so, but he should be required to make nightly advances upon the ambuscades of the devil; and every morning of his life, by way of healthful exercise, he should make a reconnoissance of the damned, having the entire control of the guerrilla rebels of the infernal regions.

EDITORIAL, JULY 6, 1861

"Shepherd, feed my sheep." This was the command of Christ to His apostles, and through them, in all time to come, to His ministers. The *nourishment* given in the earlier days of the gospel dispensation was any thing but what it is now, under the *improvements* of our age. "Repent and believe the gospel," was the first dish; "Give all diligence to make your calling and election sure," was the second *course*. The *dessert*, which was the closing out of the meal, was to the effect, that "if ye do these things ye shall never perish."[24]

Then we were not prepared to see our Southern preachers, so early as 1861, following the bad example of these *false teachers*, by preaching *Secession*, profaning the Sabbath, and taking commissions in the army to aid in carrying on a most wicked and unholy war—seeking the overthrow of the best Government the world has ever known. Ascending the sacred pulpit on the Lord's day, under a pretence of "feeding the sheep," these reverend traitors to God and their country deliver inflammatory stump-speeches, excite the worst passions of a people not extravagantly given to prayer, and thus more effectually serve the cause of the devil than all the ultra Abolition preachers of the North have been doing for a quarter of a century past. The South is now full of these reverend traitors, and every branch of the Christian Church is cursed with their labors. They can find nothing in the teachings or example of the meek and lowly Jesus to justify them in feeding

---

24. The Parson deleted here another diatribe against the northern clergy.

their flocks on the treasonable doctrines of Secession and Southern Rights, or the still more damnable heresy of the right of a State of this Union to secede at pleasure from the Federal compact, merely because a few bad men and corrupt politicians have been turned out of the Federal offices by the vote of the people.

Preachers, all must admit, have a right to their opinions and to the exercise of the right of suffrage, but they have no right to disgrace their pulpits on Sunday by delivering inflammatory stump-speeches, under the pretence of preaching Christ to the people. They have no right to abandon the congregations to whom they say God has called them to preach, and sew stripes upon their pants, swing swords to their sides, and actually turn *rowdies* in the camps of Jeff Davis! And these reverend gentlemen should remember—as very few of them do—that preachers don't make any *better* traitors than the most abandoned sinners in the country. Counterfeiting money, or forging checks upon a bank, are not less wicked acts because perpetrated by a preacher than they would be if perpetrated by an infamous gambler.

Editorial, July 6, 1861

Secession has assumed an *epidemic* form in most of the Southern States, and men become Secessionists with marvellous rapidity. It is nothing to know that a particular man was a Union man last night: how is he this morning? This is the question, and where *inducements* are held out to fall in with the heresy, it is well to inquire of men, morning, evening, and at noon, where they stand upon this great office-and-money question. Men change in a night. Men rise up and dress as Union men, and turn Secessionists before breakfast is over. The worst symptom is the morbid excitement of the organ of credulity. The cry of a loss of one's *rights* originates the disease, and it never abates till the patient "goes clear out." If a man is pressed for money, and some one in favor of "immediate separation" has some to lend *on time*, the man wanting to borrow sees that our only safety is in "a united South." If a man is a Union mechanic, and out of work, the furnishing him with a small job at once discloses the startling fact that Lincoln commenced this war, that it is a war of conquest, and that the sacred soil of the South is to be invaded and the negroes all set at liberty. The malady is short; the disease runs its course in twenty-four hours, and the patient heads a committee to order better men than himself to leave the State in a given time. He believes every lie he hears, and swears to the truth of every lie he tells. He drinks mean whiskey, and associates with men whom the day before he would have scorned. The disease is contagious, and a clever man will contract it by drinking mean whiskey out of the same tumbler with one afflicted with it.

EDITORIAL, JULY 6, 1861

We find in Secession papers some of the most notoriously false dispatches ever published in the world. These appear frequently, under sensation heads, displayed in large capitals, and with exclamation-points. We never copy them; and the reason is that we are satisfied that they do not contain a word of truth. They have turned out to be false, and, as a natural result, they have destroyed public confidence in these Secession sensation dispatches. Usually, they carry the lie upon their faces, representing a few hundred Southern troops as whipping several thousand Yankees, killing and wounding so many, while nobody is hurt on the Confederate side. To listen to the "loud-swelling words" uttered by these men, one would suppose that a regiment of Yankees will take to flight upon seeing one Southern man in uniform. We never give these exciting dispatches to our readers, and for the reason, we repeat, that we do not believe one word they set forth, and do not wish to humbug our readers, many of whom take no journal but ours.

EDITORIAL, AUGUST 10, 1861

We are informed that one of the pastors of our city actually appointed a prayer-meeting last Sabbath night to especially pray for the raising of the blockade, and that he called on God, in fervent prayer, to strike Lincoln's ships with lightning and scatter them to the four winds of heaven! The idea of a Secession preacher heaving and setting at a throne of grace—like a ram at a gate-post—asking God to raise Lincoln's blockade, is a bright idea and a rich conception, in our judgment. That churches throughout the country have become demoralized, that preachers have prostituted themselves, for Secession, is as plain as the nose on a man's face; but it does not yet appear that the Almighty has mixed Himself up with any such scenes.[25]

This parson was *Rev. Mr. Harrison*, pastor of the First Presbyterian Church in Knoxville. He held his prayer-meeting, and, assisted by several old *clericals*, made a desperate effort to raise the blockade! God, in answer to their prayer, gave them a lift on Roanoke Island [North Carolina], some weeks after the prayer-meeting, when the entire Rebel forces were either killed or taken prisoners by [Union general Ambrose E.] Burnside's blockading squadron [actually an amphibious assault force].

This man *Harrison* is the same preacher who boasted in his pulpit that Jesus Christ was a *Southerner*, born on Southern soil, and so were His apostles, except Judas, whom he denominated a *Northern* man! Speaking of the Bible, he said he would sooner have a Bible printed and bound in hell, than one printed and bound north of Mason & Dixon's line!

EDITORIAL, OCTOBER 12, 1861

To arms! to arms! ye brave!! Come, Tennesseans! ye who are the advocates of Southern rights, for separation and for Disunion—ye who have lost your rights, and feel willing to uphold the glorious flag of the South in opposition to the Hessians arrayed under the despot Lincoln—come to your country's rescue! Our gallant Governor, who led off in this State in the praiseworthy object of breaking up the old rickety Government in the hands of the Black Republicans, calls for thirty thousand volunteers, in addition to the fifty-five thousand already in the field. Shall we have them? If they do not volunteer, we shall have our State disgraced by a *draft*, and then we must go under compulsion. Come, gentlemen! Many of you have promised that "when it becomes necessary" you will turn out. That time has come, and the *necessity* is upon us. Let us show our *faith* by our *works*. We have talked long and

25. Here Brownlow deleted the concluding sentence of the original editorial and added the following two paragraphs identifying the Knoxville minister he wrote of.

loud about fighting the Union-shriekers and the Vandal hordes under the despot Lincoln. Now we have an opening. Some of us have even said we were willing for our sons to turn out and fight Union men. We have a chance at a terrible array of Unionists in Kentucky: let us volunteer, and [Confederate] General [Albert] Sidney Johnston will either lead us on to victory or something else! Come, ye braves, turn out, and let the world see that you are in earnest in making war upon the enemies of the South! Many of you have made big speeches in favor of the war; not a few of you have sought to sell the army supplies; and thousands of you are willing to stoop to fill the *offices* for the salaries they pay, and you have been so patriotic as to try to get your sons and other relations into offices. Some of you have *hired yourselves out as spies, under-strappers*, and *tools* in the glorious cause, at two to four dollars per day. Come, now, enter the ranks, as there is more honor in serving as a private. Come, gentlemen, *do* come, we insist, and enter the army as volunteers. You will feel bad when *drafted*, and pointed out as one who had to be *driven* into the service of your country! Let these Union traitors submit to the draft, but let us who are true Southern men *volunteer*. Any of us are willing to be judges, attorneys, clerks, Senators, Congressmen, and camp-followers for *pay*, when out of danger; but who of us are willing to shoulder our knapsacks and muskets and meet the Hessians? Come, gentlemen: the eyes of the people are upon you, and they want to see if you will pitch in. This is a good opening!

EDITORIAL, OCTOBER 19, 1861

We hope that our Secession neighbors will not become vexed at us for urging them to the discharge of a most serious obligation. The Governor of their choice, who has led the way in precipitating this State into rebellion, has called for an addition of thirty thousand volunteers. The men who ought to lead the way, who have been most noisy in the defence of a Southern Confederacy and of a war for independence, stand back, refuse to move a peg, and even allow those who have entered the army to come from the field of battle, where their services are actually needed, to raise companies. This is a shame! We have not less than a half-dozen gentlemen in this town, besides some in the county, who are willing to serve as members of the Confederate Congress; but not one of them proposes to raise a company or regiment, or even to serve as a private in the grand army of the South, struggling for independence! These men, moreover, are in comfortable circumstances, and could leave their families enough to live on. Not so with the poor laborers and mechanics they are urging to turn out. Their wives and children during a hard winter would be obliged to suffer.

We have several citizens who have actually been appointed to offices by the Confederate Government—say *four* of them—in this town, civil offices, that pay good salaries. Now, if these will lay aside their offices and enter the army, we shall in all time to come give them credit for a proper amount of patriotism. Let them undergo the privations of camp-life and the dangers and exposures of the battle-field, and, our word for it, the people of all parties will say they are in earnest. What do you say, gentlemen—you who hold offices, and you who are seeking offices? Let the strife and struggle for the accumulation of fortunes and posts of honor subside until this war is brought to an end. Let us show our *"faith"* by our *works"*; let us moderate our desires to make money and to fill positions of honor removed from all danger, and contribute to the general weal by the *example* of entering the service. Our ostentatious display of large subscriptions to the cause will make no lasting impression in our favor, as long as we refuse to submit to personal exposures where armies meet.

Come, gentlemen; we must insist upon your entering the service, and upon your doing it *now*. Hundreds are standing off to see if you will make good your promise to turn out *"whenever it became necessary."* It is necessary now, and the call is made from headquarters. If your section is not more prompt, not a single regiment will be made up under this last call, and a *draft* will be resorted to, which the whole South will regard as a disgrace to the "Volunteer State."

EDITORIAL, OCTOBER 26, 1861[26]

An officer accompanying some troops from Mississippi informed us that men, unknown to him, but looking like citizens, advised the

26. The date is incorrectly given as July 6 in the original text.

troops, while changing cars at Chattanooga, to mob *us* on their arrival at Knoxville. Two young soldiers, associated with our sons in Emory & Henry College, said similar advice was given to some of the Louisiana troops by officials on the railroad between Chattanooga and Knoxville. And it is a well-ascertained fact that citizens of this town have repeatedly urged the same thing upon troops, and have sought to do so when they found them under the influence of ardent spirits.

These unmitigated cowards, God-forsaken scoundrels, hell-deserving villains, and black-hearted assassins and murderers, seek to induce strangers in the army to take up quarrels and fight battles which they themselves are too cowardly to fight. For years we have held up a portion of these unprincipled dastards, dishonest, lying, swindling scoundrels, and revolting hypocrites, to the scorn, contempt, and hatred of honest men, passing and re-passing them, day by day, and it never occurred to the loathsome villains that they ought to resent it, until an opportunity offered to hide behind some infuriated troops, made drunk for the occasion. Some of them are white-livered cowards, who live by lying and swindling; others are cloaking their deceit, adultery, and numerous acts of baseness in one or another of the Churches, under a pretence of being religious; and others of them are acting for pay, as the tools of men of position and property. The superiors of many of these men in honor are in the penitentiary; and the superiors of others of them in morals and piety are in hell!

Editorial, October 26, 1861[27]

This issue of the *Whig* must necessarily be the last for some time to come: I am unable to say how long. The Confederate authorities have determined upon my arrest, and I am to be indicted before the Grand Jury of the Confederate Court, which commenced its session in Nashville on Monday last. I would have awaited the indictment and arrest before announcing the remarkable event to the world, but, as I only publish a weekly paper, my hurried removal to Nashville would deprive me of the privilege of saying to my subscribers what is alike due to myself and them. I have the fact of my indictment and consequent

---

27. Brownlow incorrectly gives this date as October 24 in the original.

arrest having been agreed upon for this week, from distinguished citizens, legislators, and lawyers at Nashville, of both parties. Gentlemen of high positions, and members of the Secession party, say that the indictment will be made because of "some treasonable articles in late numbers of the *Whig*." I have reproduced those two "treasonable articles" on the first page of this issue, that the unbiased people of the country may "read, mark, learn, and inwardly digest" the treason.[28] They relate to the culpable remissness of these Knoxville leaders in failing to volunteer in the cause of the Confederacy.

According to the usages of the court, as heretofore established, I presume I could go free, by taking the oath these authorities are administering to other Union men; but my settled purpose is not to do any such thing. I can doubtless be allowed my personal liberty, by entering into bonds to keep the peace and to demean myself toward the leaders of Secession in Knoxville, who have been seeking to have me assassinated all summer and fall, as they desire me to do; for this is really the import of the thing, and one of the leading objects sought to be attained. Although I could give a bond for my good behavior, for one hundred thousand dollars, signed by fifty as good men as the county affords, I shall obstinately refuse to do even that; and if such a bond be drawn up and signed by others, I will render it null and void by refusing to sign it. In default of both, I expect to go to jail, and I am ready to start upon one moment's warning. Not only so, but there I am prepared to lie in solitary confinement until I waste away because of imprisonment or die from old age. Stimulated by a consciousness of innocent uprightness, I will submit to imprisonment for life, or die at the end of a rope, before I will make any humiliating concession to any power on earth!

I have committed no offence. I have not shouldered arms against the Confederate Government, or the State, or encouraged others to do so. I have discouraged rebellion, publicly and privately. I have not assumed a hostile attitude toward the civil or military authorities of this new Government. But I have committed grave, and, I really fear, unpardonable offences. I have refused to make war upon the Govern-

28. These are the editorials of October 12 and 19, reprinted herein.

ment of the United States; I have refused to publish to the world false
and exaggerated accounts of the several engagements had between the
contending armies; I have refused to write out and publish false ver-
sions of the origin of this war, and of the breaking up of the best Government the world ever knew; and all this I will continue to do, if it
cost me my life. Nay, when I agree to do such things, may a righteous
God palsy my right arm, and may the earth open and close in upon me
forever!

The real object of my arrest and contemplated imprisonment is to
dry up, break down, silence, and destroy the last and only Union paper
left in the eleven seceded States, and thereby to keep from the people
of East Tennessee the facts which are daily transpiring in the country.
After the Hon. Jeff Davis had stated in Richmond, in a conversation
relative to my paper, that he would not live in a Government that did
not tolerate freedom of the press—after the judges, attorneys, jurors,
and all others filling positions of honor or trust under the "permanent
Constitution," which guarantees *freedom of the press*—and after the entire press of the South had come down in their thunder tones upon the
Federal Government for suppressing the Louisville *Courier* and the
New York *Day-Book*, and other Secession journals—I did expect the
utmost liberty to be allowed to one small sheet, whose errors could be
combated by the entire Southern press! It is not enough that my paper
has been denied a circulation through the ordinary channels of convey-
ance in the country, but it must be discontinued altogether, or its editor
must write and select only such articles as meet the approval of a pack
of scoundrels in Knoxville, when their superiors in all the qualities
that adorn human nature are in the penitentiary of our State! And this
is the boasted liberty of the press in the Southern Confederacy!

I shall in no degree feel humbled by being cast into prison, whenever
it is the will and pleasure of this august Government to put me there;
but, on the contrary, I shall feel proud of my confinement. I shall go to
jail—as John Rogers went to the stake[29]—for my *principles*. I shall go,
because I have failed to recognize the hand of God in the work of

29. John Rogers was a Protestant preacher executed in 1555 after Queen Mary I re-
stored Catholicism in England.

breaking up the American Government, and the inauguration of the most wicked, cruel, unnatural, and uncalled-for war ever recorded in history. I go, because I have refused to laud to the skies the acts of tyranny, usurpation, and oppression inflicted upon the people of East Tennessee for their devotion to the Constitution and laws of the Government handed down to them by their fathers, and the liberties secured to them by a war of seven long years of gloom, poverty, and trial! I repeat, I am proud of my position and of my principles, and shall leave them to my children as a legacy far more valuable than a princely fortune, had I the latter to bestow!

With me life has lost some of its energy: having passed six annual posts on the western slope of half a century, something of the fire of youth is exhausted; but I stand forth with the eloquence and energy of right to sustain and stimulate me in the maintenance of my principles. I am encouraged to firmness when I look back to the fate of Him "whose power was righteousness," while the infuriated mob cried out, "Crucify him! crucify him!"

I owe to my numerous list of subscribers the filling out of their respective terms for which they have made advance payments, and, if circumstances ever place it in my power to discharge these obligations, I will do it most certainly. But if I am denied the liberty of doing so, they must regard their small losses as so many contributions to the cause in which I have fallen. I feel that I can with confidence rely upon the magnanimity and forbearance of my patrons under this state of things. They will bear me witness that I have held out as long as I am allowed to, and that I have yielded to a military despotism that I could not avert the horrors of or successfully oppose.

I will only say, in conclusion—for I am not allowed the privilege to write—that the people of this country have been unaccustomed to such wrongs; they can yet scarcely realize them. They are astounded for the time-being with the quick succession of outrages that have come upon them, and they stand horror-stricken, like men expecting ruin and annihilation. I may not live to see the day, but thousands of my readers will, when the people of this once prosperous country will see that they are marching by "double-quick time" from freedom to bondage. They will then look these wanton outrages upon right and liberty full in the face, and my prediction is that they will "stir the stones of Rome to rise and mutiny." Wrongs less wanton and outrageous precipitated the French Revolution. Citizens cast into dungeons without charges of crime against them, and without the formalities of a trial by jury; private property confiscated at the beck of those in power; the press humbled, muzzled, and suppressed, or prostituted to serve the ends of tyranny! The crimes of Louis XVI fell short of all this, and yet he lost his head! The people of this country, down-trodden and oppressed, still have the resolution of their illustrious forefathers, who asserted their rights at Lexington and Bunker Hill!

Exchanging, with proud satisfaction, the editorial chair and the sweet endearments of home for a cell in the prison or the lot of an exile,

I have the honor to be, &c.,

WILLIAM G. BROWNLOW,
Editor of the Knoxville Whig[30]

30. After publishing this issue of the *Whig*, Brownlow closed his office and, in early November, left Knoxville. His subsequent adventures are narrated in Part IV.

III

ESSAY ON EAST TENNESSEE

†

EAST TENNESSEE—as loyal to this Government as any State in the Union—is composed of thirty large counties, and is really as separate and distinct from Middle and West Tennessee as any of the adjoining States are. It is a valley three hundred miles in length, and varying in width from fifty to seventy-five miles. It is separated from Kentucky, on the north, by the range of mountains known as Cumberland Mountains, extending westward and southwestward, and lying between the great valley of East Tennessee and the Cumberland River, one of the largest affluents—the Tennessee excepted—of the Ohio, rising among the mountains in the southeast portion of Kentucky. The Cumberland range of mountains belongs to the Appalachian chain, and extends the whole length of the great valley of East Tennessee. Over this range of mountains, through its dense groves and interminable laurel-thickets, the persecuted and oppressed Union men of East Tennessee have forced their way, travelling after night and lying up in daytime, with a view of joining the Federal army, until they are now (May, 1862) organizing the *Sixth Tennessee Regiment*, determined to fight back to their homes and families.

On the south, East Tennessee is separated from North Carolina and Georgia by the Chilhowee and Iron Mountains, and by the Allegheny Mountains, extending in a continuous chain from Virginia to Georgia and Alabama. This range of mountains forms a dividing-line between Eastern and Western Virginia, and makes East Tennessee and Southwestern Virginia one country, identical in interest, as they are one in soil, climate, and productions.

The population of East Tennessee partakes of the same parentage as that of Kentucky, the original settlers having been mostly from North

Carolina and Virginia; and they are second to no people for manly frankness of character, courage, and loyalty to the Federal Government. There are fewer slaves in East Tennessee than in any other portion of the State of equal extent; and, as a general thing, the people are very much upon an equality as to their possessions.

The face of the country in East Tennessee is very agreeably diversified with mountain, hill, and plain, containing within its limits much fertility of soil, great beauty of scenery, and a delightfully temperate climate. The hills are wooded to their tops with every variety of timber, whilst on all the small rivers and large creeks there are embosomed delightful and fertile valleys of farming-lands, in a high state of cultivation. Many of the uplands are very level, and others, generally undulating, are very productive. I have resided there for more than thirty years, and have explored every one of the thirty counties. And if there lives a man, old or young, in East Tennessee who is more extensively acquainted with the inhabitants than I am, I have never made his acquaintance.

The climate of East Tennessee is mild. Considerable snow sometimes falls in the winter, which, however, is generally short, and does not allow of snow lying on the ground long. During the winter of 1861–2 there was but one light snow, and up to the time of my leaving (3d of March) there had not been a formation of ice to the thickness of half an inch! The summers are free from the intense heat of the Gulf States, and, as a consequence, many families come from the South to spend the summers at the valuable mineral springs, which are found in great abundance; and many of them are handsomely improved.

East Tennessee is not a cotton-growing country, but is favorable alone to grazing; and great numbers of livestock—horses, mules, cattle, hogs, and sheep—are exported from thence to the Atlantic States. Indian corn and wheat are the great staples. Besides these, rye, oats, buckwheat, potatoes (sweet and Irish), wool, flax, and hay, are produced in great abundance. Apples and peaches, pears and plums, grow to great perfection. Maple-sugar is made of a fine quality, also superior butter and cheese. It is, in one word, the Switzerland of America; and I do not intend to be driven out of it by the more-than-savage beasts who now have it in possession.

The Holston River courses through the entire valley of East Tennessee, and is navigable for steamboats nine months in the year. Its tributaries above Knoxville are Pigeon, French Broad, Chucky, and Watauga Rivers. Below Knoxville, it receives Little River, Clinch, Hiwassee, and [Little] Tennessee, and at the confluence of this last stream loses its name, and is called the Tennessee River until its junction with the Ohio—a distance of about seven hundred miles. Gold has been found in considerable quantities, but the most abundant metallic minerals are iron, copper, zinc, and lead. Of the earthy minerals, coal of a superior quality is abundant in all the counties bordering on the Cumberland Mountains. There are also gypsum of a fine quality, beautiful varieties of marble, nitre, slate, and salt. The abundance of accessible iron-ore, bituminous coal, and water-power is beginning to attract the attention of capitalists. A railroad is in a forward state of construction, extending from Knoxville to the coal and iron banks at the foot of the Cumberland Mountains, and intended to connect with Kentucky and Cincinnati. Thirty miles of this road are graded, and a portion of the track is laid; and, but for this war and the blockade, it would have been in use to the foot of the mountain.

Knoxville, a flourishing city, the capital of Knox county, the great metropolis of East Tennessee, was the first seat of the State Government, where Governor Blount resided.[1] It is beautifully situated, upon a succession of hills, on the right bank of Holston River, four miles below its confluence with the French Broad, *two hundred and sixty miles* from Nashville by railroad, and *two hundred* by the old stage-road. The town was laid out in 1794. It contains the State Asylum for the Deaf and Dumb, and is the seat of the University of East Tennessee, an institution chartered in 1807. It has a population of some six thousand, exhibits an aspect of increasing prosperity, and manufactures of various kinds are springing up in its vicinity. It has seven churches, and quite a number of stores, some of them very fine. It has three banks, and at present but *one* newspaper, and that a vile Secession journal, edited by a scoundrel, debauchee, and coward named

1. William Blount was actually the territorial governor of Tennessee, from 1790 until statehood was granted in 1796. Knoxville was the capital both during the territorial period and in the early years of statehood.

[J. Austin] *Sperry*, selected by a more unprincipled set of men than he is himself, because of his *adaptation* to the dirty work he is employed to do. . . .

The Federal Government owes it to the loyal people of East Tennessee to send an army there and liberate that oppressed and downtrodden population. If it shall never accomplish any thing more, it ought at least, and at any cost of money and blood, to do that much. I have confidence in the Government doing this thing, and at no very distant day. When this is done, I desire to return to my family and former field of labor, and again edit and publish my paper.

It is the interest of the Government to take possession of that important field. The Rebel authorities have slaughtered several hundred thousand hogs there, and have a corresponding number of beef-cattle pickled up, and a quantity of wheat and flour on hand. The East Tennessee and Georgia Railroad extends from Knoxville to Chattanooga and Dalton, a distance of one hundred and thirty miles, and connects with Augusta, Montgomery, Memphis, and Nashville. Going east from Knoxville, the railroad extends to Lynchburg, and connects with Manassas, Richmond, Petersburg, and Norfolk; and from the beginning of this infamous rebellion this great line of railroad gave new impetus to the Rebel movements, pouring a stream of Secession fire into Virginia from the Cotton States. Indeed, it has been a matter of surprise that our army did not march upon East Tennessee long ago, capture Knoxville, and take possession of that great railroad. It was certainly owing to bad generalship in Kentucky, as there are several gaps through which the approach could be made. The Pound Gap is one, about a hundred miles east of Knoxville, and about opposite to Bristol, on the line between Virginia and Tennessee. Another gap is the one at Jim Town, about eighty miles northwest of Knoxville, and near where the celebrated battle of Fishing Creek [Kentucky] was fought [on January 19, 1862]. After the fall of [Confederate] General [Felix K.] Zollicoffer, and the disgraceful *run* made by the Rebel troops, one regiment of Federal troops could have taken and held Knoxville. And so certain were the Secession leaders that it would be done, that many of them packed up their effects and fled into Georgia.

Cumberland Gap—a very remarkable formation—is only sixty-five miles northeast of Knoxville, and only about forty miles from this great railroad. The mountain-range trends to the south, the road through the gap running nearly east-and-west. On the left of the road, looking from the Tennessee side, is a very high mountain—I should say, more than two thousand feet above the plain—terminating very abruptly at the gap, which is simply a depression, say about one thousand feet lower than the extreme high point. On the right of the gap the mountain rises about two hundred feet, and trends southeast, nearly four or five miles.

When I left home, the 3d of March, there were seven thousand [Confederate] troops there, under the command of Colonel [James E.] Rains; and they, as I am informed, have been reinforced, and are under the command of General E. Kirby Smith, late from the Potomac. But the Rebels stationed there all the fall and winter were undisciplined troops, and poorly armed with such squirrel-guns and shot-guns as were taken from the Union men. Their cannon are small, not equalling, by any means, those used by the Federal army. The position could be made very strong, but it is by no means impregnable, with men forced into the Rebel service from the Union ranks and unwilling to fight against the Stars and Stripes. The men living round about there, and for many miles up and down the valley, are on the side of the Union, and would flock to the standard of the Federal army as soon as they would appear in force.

The Federal army will cross there this spring or summer, and I shall not be at all surprised if the Rebels evacuate the place and fall back upon Knoxville. In that event, a stand and fight will be made at Knoxville.

When East Tennessee came to vote herself out of the Union, she showed her loyalty and did herself honor. The election was first held in February [1861], under the proclamation of the Governor, and all voters were to write on their tickets *Convention* or *No Convention*, and if the Convention carried, the delegates chosen at the same time would assemble. For *No Convention* there were 70,000 votes cast as against 50,000, and but *three* Secessionists elected in the State.

The following is the vote of glorious EAST TENNESSEE: [34,000 for no convention, 7,550 for convention]. . . .

Failing to call an election of delegates to Nashville by the people, and failing to get a Convention sanctioned, the Governor [on April 18, 1861] called an extra session of the Legislature; and that body, in violation of the expressed will of the people, declared an ordinance of separation on the 6th of May, submitting the questions of *separation* from the Federal Government and of *representation* in the Richmond Congress to be voted on by the people on the 8th day of June. By rushing Rebel bayonets into East Tennessee from the Cotton States, and by intimidating thousands and running rough-shod over others, the State was forced out of the Union, when a majority of her people were utterly averse to any such separation. Frauds were perpetrated at the ballot-box, timid men were kept from the polls, and thousands were allowed to vote who had no right to do so under the laws and Constitution of the State. . . .

For separation and representation at Richmond, East Tennessee gave 14,700 votes; and half of that number were Rebel troops, having no authority under the Constitution to vote at any election. For *no separation* and *no representation*—the straight-out Union vote—East Tennessee gave 33,000, or 18,300 of a majority, with at least 5,000 quiet citizens deterred from coming out by threats of violence, and by the presence of drunken troops at the polls to insult them.

To aid in forcing the State out, the votes of *pretended* Tennesseans were taken at the different military camps in and out of the State. . . .

By such fraud and villainy as this, the great State of Tennessee was carried out of the Union. The loyal people of East Tennessee, to their great honor, had no lot or part in the work. The Union men of the State are now in the majority, and will have the State back or die in the last ditch!

IV

NARRATIVE:
IMPRISONMENT, RELEASE,
AND TRAVELS

†

Much of what now follows was written down by the author in small blank-books, with a pencil, in the Knoxville jail, and in a private room, while the outer doors were guarded with Rebel bayonets. That portion given in the form of a *journal* will be transmitted to posterity just as it was written down at the time, and without any attempt at polish. When most of these sketches reach the eyes of my prison-companions in the Knoxville jail, they will recall to them our mutual sufferings, and they will readily attest the truthfulness of my narrative. They will at once bear testimony as to the fidelity of my descriptions and the accuracy with which I have stated facts, although they will regret that I have not gone more into detail.

Whilst I desire to let the world see what the real *spirit* of Secession is in the South, and to expose the guilty leaders to the scorn and contempt of all coming generations, I wish to enlist the interests and sympathies of all who may find leisure to peruse these pages. I have known, during my darkest hour of trial, that I had the sympathies of all good citizens in the loyal States, and did not doubt that thousands of devout prayers were offered up for my preservation and ultimate release, and for the safety and release of the innocent Union men confined with me and in other jails. If in these pages I can vindicate my consistency and satisfy the public that their sympathies have been merited, I will have accomplished all that is desired or aimed at by the publication of them.

When the storm arose in the South—say a little over twelve months ago—and the current set in seemingly favorable to Secession, vast numbers rushed into their ranks, actuated by the worst motives that ever governed the actions of as many bad men—the daring and improvident, the indolent, the thoughtless, the bankrupts of the country, and the thousands indebted to Northern merchants, debauched members of the churches, apostate preachers, and the intemperate—all the loose elements of society in the towns and villages—those who were reckless of consequences, and to whom no change could be productive of injury—men who really had every thing to gain and nothing to lose, even by so violent and destructive a revolution.

And whilst many of the substantial men of the country entered the army—for the most part as officers, contractors, wagon-masters, and furnishers of supplies in various forms—a much greater number entered the service who were pusillanimous and worthless, lazy and sensual, having no visible means of support. Many of these were known to me in East Tennessee and other portions of the South; and I can safely say that when they entered the service, and were fitted out with suits of coarse jeans and supplied with army-rations, they were better dressed and fed than they ever had been before. Not a few of these entered the Rebel service with a view to get rid of their wives and children, who were looking to them for a support, and whose bread and meat were guaranteed by those who urged them to volunteer, but who, after they were gone, left their families to shift for themselves.

It was a common thing to hear men of this class, dressed in uniform, and under the influence of mean whiskey, swearing upon the streets that they intended to have their rights, or kill the last Lincolnite north of Mason & Dixon's line! Ask one of them what rights he had lost and was so vehemently contending for, and the reply would be, the right to carry his negroes into the Territories. At the same time, the man never owned a negro in his life, and never was related, by consanguinity or affinity, to any one who did own a negro! Nay, I have heard captains of Rebel companies bluster in this way, who could not get credit in a Secession store for a pair of shoes or a pound of coffee.

And, as if resolved to keep up a show of consistency and carry out the same spirit, society was disjointed, and was everywhere thrown into the loosest state in which it could exist, upon the inauguration of Secession. There were no regular magistrates, no laws, no judges, no tribunals to protect the weak and innocent or to punish the guilty. Take for example the case of a Union man in Knox county, who was tied upon a log, his back stripped bare, and cut all to pieces with hickories, as one of my engravings will show. When he was brought into the court-house, and his back exhibited, he was told that these were revolutionary times, and that he had no remedy. Every man had to assert his own rights and avenge his own wrongs, or, as most were compelled to do, submit to insult and injury. Squads of six and ten Rebel troops, upon their own responsibilities, scoured the country, arrested whom they chose, and treated them as their malice and beastly habits of life suggested. Take the case of Captain *Bill Brown*, of Bradley county, who, at the head of a company of cavalry, arrested Union men, and forced from them sums of money to pay him for their release, until he boasted of having two thousand dollars. This charge was brought before the military authorities at Knoxville, and again dismissed without a reproof to this robber.

As a general thing, these outlaws, who were operating all over East Tennessee, were neither restrained by a sense of shame, the dictates of humanity, nor the fear of God. Hence, many innocent persons fell victims to their malevolence, and had their property either shamefully abused or recklessly destroyed. Tennessee is a greatly-damaged State—thousands of the men having escaped into Kentucky, leaving their homes and crops, all of which have since been destroyed by the Rebel troops. This is especially so in the several counties along the south side of the Cumberland Mountains. Kentucky and Missouri will both feel the effects of this devastating war—a war which the Cotton States artfully contrived to transfer to the border States, but which, thanks to the energy of the heads of the Federal army, is falling back to where it ought to have begun, and where it should end. . . .

Early in the spring of 1861 a stream of Secession fire began to pour through East Tennessee, along the great [East] Tennessee & Virginia Railroad, and troops were rushed along the road in greater numbers than the rolling stock upon the road would afford facilities for transporting. These regiments, coming from the Cotton States, and many of them *vagabonds* and *wharf-rats* from New Orleans, Mobile, and Texas, were brimfull of prejudice against me and my paper. These prejudices were increased and their malice inflamed by the falsehoods related to them by unprincipled citizens and cowards whom I had de-

Rebels whipping a man for expressing Union sentiments.

nounced for years, and by certain railroad-employés on their way to Knoxville. Hence, after they would arrive in Knoxville and pay a visit to the whiskey-shops, they would forthwith swarm around my print-ing-office and dwelling-house, howl like wolves, swear oaths that would blister the lips of a sailor, blackguard my family, and threaten to demolish my house, and even to hang me. This was kept up the en-tire summer and fall, and increased in violence until my paper was suppressed and my office seized upon and occupied by the Rebel mili-tary authorities—which was in November last.

While General Zollicoffer remained at Knoxville in command, I was protected, and so were all other Union men and their families. Previous to his coming, however, certain officers of [John C.] Vaughn's regiment of East Tennessee Volunteers commenced personal violence on Union men, and occasioned a row in the street, shooting down a *Mr. Ball*, and firing several shots at *Charles S. Douglas*—the man who ran up the Union flag on Gay Street and protected it with a double-barrel shot-gun—one shot slightly wounding him in the neck. The next day certain of these officers came into town from camps, in a close carriage, entered the hotel at the ladies' entrance, and watched for Douglas from a window until he appeared at his window on the oppo-site side of the street, when they took deliberate aim at him and shot him through the breast with a large musket-ball. Thus was Douglas murdered in a most cowardly and brutal manner, while the State was a member of the Federal Union; and the circuit court judge and the State's Attorney were both in town, but, being Secessionists, no bill was sent against the murderers of Douglas, nor was one word said in court on the subject; but his widow and one small child were left to take care of themselves. Nor is this all. The Episcopal minister, Mr. Hames, was proscribed for daring to attend the funeral and officiate, at the request of the widow. This is the *spirit* which has characterized this rebellion throughout the South!

After the departure of General Zollicoffer to Cumberland Gap, I soon became convinced that I was in danger of personal violence from the soldiers left there under the command of one *Rev. Colonel W. B. Wood*, of Alabama, a hypocrite, who preached in the Methodist Church on Sunday and the next day encouraged his men to do acts of violence. Certain of these troops were in the habit of coming daily to my residence, or passing by it, flourishing their large knives, pointing their guns at the windows, and threatening to take my life. They were incited to act in this manner by my bitter personal enemies and by the cowardly miscreant who conducted the rebel organ in Knoxville, and who desired me and my paper out of their way. They were also encouraged by this unmitigated villain, *Parson Colonel Wood*. My enemies seeking to make the military the instruments of their private revenge, and my condition becoming more and more perilous each day, my family became convinced that my life was in danger, as did other friends, and all believed that my presence at home imperilled instead of securing the safety of my wife and children. I therefore yielded to the entreaties of my family and friends to leave home for a time, and I consented to do so the more readily as I had debts owing to me in the adjoining counties of Blount, Sevier, Cocke, and Grainger, for advertising. I accordingly left home the first week in November, on horseback, in company with Rev. James Cumming, and whilst I was still in Blount—less than thirty miles from home—the bridges on the railroad were destroyed by fire.[1] My absence at the time was seized upon as evidence of my complicity in the matter, although I was not nearer than one day's ride of the railroad, and on Sunday, the day after the burning, I preached to a large congregation in Sevierville.

But the most intense excitement prevailed in the country after the news was circulated; harangues were delivered in the towns and military camps, and the passions of the Secession citizens and of the soldiers were inflamed; and my knowledge of the history of mankind in the past taught me that in such seasons of high excitement the innocent and the guilty would suffer together. Meanwhile, I learned, by express-riders friendly to me, that this vile man Wood had sent out scouts of cavalry after me in different directions, with instructions,

1. On the night of November 8, 1861, bands of Unionist saboteurs struck at the railroad running through East Tennessee, burning several bridges. The plot had been approved and financed by top federal officials in Washington, and was supposed to be supported by a Union military invasion of East Tennessee. The northern army failed to materialize, however, and in the subsequent Confederate crackdown hundreds of suspected bridge-burners were arrested and five hanged.

publicly given them on the street, not to take me a prisoner, but to shoot me down upon sight. Military law was declared in Knoxville; the city was guarded, and those who escaped from the city to give me word had to cross the river after night in a canoe. In this state of things, prudence dictated that I should for a time conceal myself from the gaze of these bloodhounds and authorized murderers, so that no occasion should occur for violence to my person. Quite a number of us—among whom were members of the Legislature, preachers, and planters—retired into the Smoky Mountains, separating North Carolina from Tennessee, and quite beyond the precincts of civilization. Amidst the high summits of this range of mountains, and in one of their deep gorges where no vehicle had ever penetrated, we struck up camp, and for days and nights together we stayed there. Our friends from Wear's Cove conveyed provisions to us, and in the mean time one of our party killed a fat bear, which supplied us with meat. In the cove below us there was a company of "Home-Guards"—Union men— well armed, who kept a watch for our pursuers, who failed to learn our whereabouts. We were high up on the east fork of Little River, and there was but one gap through which we could have been approached, and in that event it would have required a large force to take us.

Scouts were multiplied to search for us, and we were made acquainted with that fact; and, as it was known that we were in Tuckaluchee Cove and in Wear's Cove, we deemed it prudent to disperse, and to secrete ourselves in different places, two-and-two together. I resolved upon going within six or eight miles of Knoxville, where I had Union friends who would take care of me; and, accordingly, the Rev. W. T. Dowell and myself mounted our horses at dark, having previously come down out of the mountains, and, riding something less than forty miles through the deep gorges, daylight brought us to the comfortable lodgings of a friend. Here we tarried for a time, and were put in secret communication with Knoxville, distant six miles, having removed our horses to another point. Learning that the murderous scouts of the still more bloodthirsty and despicable Wood were still after me, I addressed the following note to Brigadier-General [William H.] Carroll:

Friday, Nov. 22, 1861

GENERAL W. H. CARROLL:

Having understood that you are to be placed in command of the military post at Knoxville in a few days, I desire to lay a statement of facts before you. I left home on the 4th of this month to attend the Chancery Court in Maryville, Blount county, and to go from there to Sevierville, to collect fees due me for advertising, and in part I have succeeded. I have not been concerned in getting up an armed force to war upon your troops, as falsely reported.

I left home, and have remained absent for eighteen days, at the earnest and repeated solicitations of my family, who insisted that they would be more secure in my absence. Certain troops came daily on my portico, and, in front of my dwelling, drew out and flourished side-knives, and sometimes presented muskets, threatening my life. I was told that they were under the command of an Alabama officer by the name of *Wood*, and that he was arrayed against me.

As it regards the bridge-burning, I never had any intimation of any such purpose, from any quarter. I condemn the act, and regard it as an ill-timed measure, calculated to bring no good to any one or any party, but much harm to innocent men and to the public. When I, together with fifteen or twenty other leading Union men, signed a communication to General Zollicoffer, proposing to counsel peace, I acted in good faith; and I have kept that faith. That address has been published in all the Tennessee papers; and, had any purpose to fire the bridges been made known to me, I should have felt bound to disclose the fact to the officers of the [rail]road.

I am ready and willing at any time to stand a trial upon these or other points before any civil tribunal; but I protest against being turned over to *any infuriated mob of armed men* filled with prejudice by my bitterest enemies.

This communication will be handed to you by my friend Colonel John Williams, a man favorably known to you and the country.

I am, respectfully, &c.,

W. G. BROWNLOW

Head-Quarters, Knoxville, Nov. 28, 1861

REV. DR. BROWNLOW:

It is my business here to afford protection to all citizens who are loyal to the Confederate States; and I shall use all the force at my command to that end. You may be fully assured that you will meet with no personal violence by returning to your home; and, if you can establish what you say in your letter of the 22d inst., *you shall have every opportunity to do so before the civil tribunal, if it is necessary*—PROVIDED YOU HAVE COMMITTED NO ACT THAT WILL MAKE IT NECESSARY FOR THE MILITARY LAW TO TAKE COGNIZANCE.

I desire that every loyal citizen, regardless of former political opinions, shall be fully protected in all his rights and privileges; and to accomplish which I shall bend all my energies, and have no doubt I shall be successful.

Respectfully, &c.,

Wm. H. Carroll,
Brig.-Gen. Com.

Thursday, December 4, 1861

General W. H. Carroll:

Your letter of the 28th ult. did not reach me until the 1st inst., and I return, for an answer to the slanderous charges whispered into your ears by my cowardly enemies, touching myself and others, as the correspondents of men in Kentucky, and as *knowing* the bridges were to be burned, the following documents:

The undersigned, being charged with having and reading a letter in Maryville, during the fourth and fifth days of November past, purporting to say that the railroad-bridges were to be burned, take this method of testifying to the public that there is not one word of truth in the entire statement; that we have neither seen, handled, read, or heard read, any letter on that subject, from any quarter whatsoever. We further state, upon our oaths, that neither of us has received from, or addressed or conveyed to, any person in Kentucky, or connected with the Federal army, during the entire summer and fall, any private letter touching the war or the troubles growing out of the war. We also testify, upon our oaths, that we had no knowledge whatsoever of any purpose or plot, on the part of any persons or party, to burn the bridges: had we been apprized of such a movement, we should have protested against it as an outrage. Subscribed and sworn to this 2d of December, 1861.

James Cumming,
W. G. Brownlow,
W. T. Dowell

Personally appeared before me, an acting Justice of the Peace in and for the County of Blount and State of Tennessee, this 2d of December, 1861, James Cumming, W. G. Brownlow, and W. T. Dowell, and made oath, in due form of law, that the allegations set forth in the foregoing statement, and subscribed by them, are true.

Solomon Farmer,
Justice of the Peace for Blount County

Mr. Cumming is now in his seventy-seventh year, has all his life long sustained an unblemished character, has been a Methodist itinerant preacher for the last *forty* years, and previous to that served two campaigns under General [Andrew] Jackson, associated with your venerable father,[2] General [John] Coffee, and other patriots, in defending our *whole* country—not a part of it—against the combined assaults of our British and savage foes—undergoing the hardships of camp-life among the inhospitable swamps of Mobile and New Orleans. Indeed, he was a major in Colonel [John] Williams's regiment of Tennessee Volunteers; and that gallant officer, afterwards a Senator in Congress, bore witness to the courage and fidelity of Mr. Cumming. His character and services ought to shield him in his declining years from such slanders as are now heaped upon him, and would do it were he living anywhere else than in this so-called Southern Confederacy. But he is a Union man, opposed to the disruption of the Government he has suffered and fought for; and this is the head and front of his offending.

Mr. Dowell is a native of Alabama, but has lived nearly all his life in East Tennessee, sustaining the character of an honest man, in the counties of Anderson, Carter, Sevier, Knox, and Blount, where he is now a respectable merchant and an acceptable local preacher in the Methodist Church. But he is a Union man, loyal to the Government of the United States, and opposed to the heresy of Secession; and this is the reason why he is assailed.

So far as I am concerned, I have labored for years, in my humble way, to help build up this great line of railroads, and I can have no desire to see them destroyed. If the Federal Government succeed in recovering this country, it will need the facilities these roads afford; but if the Confederates hold the country, the roads are alike important to the citizens of all parties. No good can come to anybody from the destruction of these roads, but much harm to individuals and to the public at large.

No candid man of any party believes that I am even remotely connected with the recent burning of these bridges; but to charge it upon me, and raise a clamor through the country, affords a pretext, though flimsy it be, for seizing upon my property, as has been done, by a military mob, and appropriating it to the use of your so-called Confederacy. It was not enough that I should be refused the privilege of publishing my paper, but my press, engine, and type have been seized upon, and I am refused the privilege of selling them to procure the means of supporting a helpless family of children. Nay, my office-

2. General Carroll's father was William Carroll, governor of Tennessee, 1821–'27, and 1829–'35.

building has been taken from me, and is occupied by your military authorities, without fee or reward to me. Is this the liberty and justice offered to men by this new and better Government you are setting up? Are these the blessings of Southern Rights so much talked of? If so, God deliver me and my children from their benign influences! But, sir, what better could I expect from a bogus Government, that originated in fraud and falsehood, perjury and theft?

I have now been absent from home one month—not because I have committed any crime, but because I have desired no collision between me and the drunken and infuriated troops, urged to assault me by the cowardly villains who throng the town, and whose frauds, bad morals, and revolting crimes I have held up to public gaze. I cannot feel safe in returning, for I am not sure that your letter offers protection to me. You say it is your "business here to afford protection to *all citizens who are loyal to the Confederate States.*" If you mean by *loyalty* faithfulness and fidelity, I can scarcely hope for protection. I am loyal to the Government of the United States, and that is the only Government I consider as having an existence in this country. I have studied the Bible for many years, and I have great respect for the lessons it has taught me. One of these lessons is, that I must not attempt to serve Two Masters. I am therefore a Union man, and I must adhere to the Federal Government until that is destroyed—which I hope and trust may never be done—and then I will turn to the next best Government I can find.

I am not in arms against your Confederacy. I have not encouraged rebellion on the part of Union men, but the reverse; and I am quietly awaiting the result of the contest going on. In this *neutral* condition I feel that I ought to be let alone, and left to the quiet enjoyment of opinions I honestly entertain and cannot conscientiously surrender. *You*, but a few months ago, entertained the same opinions I do, and acted with me in opposition to Secession. Toward me, personally, I think you would entertain none but kind feelings, were you not associated with the men you are. I understand that your daily associates are *John H. Crozier, J. Crozier Ramsey*, and *W. H. Sneed.*

Crozier blames me for driving him into private life. He is a corrupt demagogue, a selfish liar, and an unmitigated coward. I have held him up to public gaze, in this threefold capacity, from the stump and through the press, before his face and behind his back, and he has never had the spirit to resent it until recently, and then only by hiding behind your volunteers and seeking to hiss them on me. He also feels *sore* under my exposure of his brother, *A. R. Crozier*, who was connected with the great swindle practised by the Bank of East Tennessee, and, after making his pile by that operation, packed up bag and baggage and cut out for Texas! The records of our Chancery Court will give you the facts in the case.

Ramsey is but a few degrees removed from an idiot. He is the nephew of the Croziers and the son of one of the directors of this villainous bank, against whom I instituted and recovered an important suit, exposing the *father*, the *uncle*, and the entire *Democratic* swindle. Young Ramsey is smarting under the part I took in helping to defeat him for the United States Congress, when he was beaten two thousand votes by Horace Maynard. Somebody once said, "That in the kingdom of the blind the one-eyed are monarchs"; and I suppose it was upon this principle, if we give the maxim a literal construction, that young Ramsey, with his "one talent," was elevated to such a pitch as to be made a Confederate Attorney by Jeff Davis!

Sneed is a noble specimen of the physical man. Corpulent, swaggering, a giant in his own estimation, his form looms up in the distance, and when he is on the street he makes the whole town know it! His whole figure exhibits a majesty of proportion, a majesty of combination, sometimes seen in the liquor-shop statues with whom he associates. His eyelashes are nearly scorched off by alcoholic fire; and nature, to keep up appearances, in a fit of desperation is substituting in their stead a binding of red, which looks like two little rainbows hanging upon a storm, such as he often passes through in the domestic circle! This man has been a candidate for all the offices of honor and profit that have come up during his long residence in East Tennessee, and never was successful but once, when he was elected to the Congress of the United States. The people then complained that he was elected through the influence of my press, for I entered heartily into his support, as he was a *Whig* and his competitor a *Democrat*. In Congress his associates were *Disunionists* and his votes were *sectional*. He was not again a candidate. Indeed, a press like mine in each of the ten counties in the district could not have re-elected him. When Secession turned up, he pitched in, and became a candidate to represent Knox county in the Convention. Out of four thousand votes polled in a single-handed contest he obtained two hundred and thirty. Since then he has been travelling in search of his rights, and swears that he will follow them on to the other side of sundown!

Whenever the Federal army shall approach Tennessee in force, Crozier, Ramsey, Sneed, and others of the same clique, will fall back into the Cotton States, and call upon the mountains and hills to hide them from the wrath of the Union men in East Tennessee whom they have persecuted, insulted, and sought to have murdered by your drunken and infuriated troops. These are certainly accomplished and erudite reformers of our National Government! Mark my prediction: these men will take to their heels upon the approach of one regiment of Federal troops. I know the men and have studied their characters. I may not be living when a Federal army enters East Tennessee, but if I am living next spring, I expect to enjoy the luxury. If this be treason, make the most of it!

As this letter to you is private, General, and as you were until recently a Union man, you must allow me to deal candidly with you. I have no idea that you approve this Secession movement, but feel certain that in your heart you despise the whole affair. As long as I see the *spirit* of the rebellion acted out by your leaders, and as long as I bear in mind the *characters* of the men who originated it, I can but despise the whole concern and desire its overthrow. I may not be gratified with seeing this rebellion put down, but my children will; and, if I am not assassinated by the hired tools of some of your new associates, I will live to see the rebellion closed out, and not be more than *one year* older than I now am!

I am, sir, &c.,

W. G. BROWNLOW

My friend, who was in charge of the foregoing letter, withheld it from General Carroll, on account of the following epistles, intended for me, and of the existence of which I had no knowledge at the time I wrote the one of the 4th of December:

Head-Quarters, Knoxville, Tenn., Dec. 4, 1861

W. G. BROWNLOW, ESQ.:

The Major-General commanding directs me to say that upon calling at his head-quarters, within twenty-four hours, you can get a passport to go into Kentucky, accompanied by a military escort, the route to be designated by General [George B.] Crittenden.

I am, sir, very respectfully, your obedient servant,

A. S. CUNNINGHAM,
Acting Adjutant-General

The following letter, a copy of which I was furnished with on the day and date of the foregoing, seems to have been withheld, or, at least, not acted upon, for ten days:

Confederate States of America,
War Department, Richmond, Nov. 20, 1861

To Major-General Crittenden:

Dear Sir: I have been asked to grant a passport for Brownlow, to leave the State of Tennessee. He is said to have secreted himself, fearing violence to his person, and to be anxious to depart from the State.

I cannot give him a formal passport, though I would greatly prefer seeing him on the other side of our lines, *as an avowed enemy.* I wish, however, to say that I would be glad to learn that he has left Tennessee; and I have no objection to interpose to his leaving, if you are willing to let him pass.

Yours, truly,

J. P. Benjamin,
Secretary of War

It turned out, upon examination, that Colonel [John] Baxter, of Knoxville, a moderate Secessionist, was in Richmond at the time Mr. Benjamin wrote to General Crittenden, and made this application without my knowledge. He was doubtless influenced by two motives—one of friendship to me and my family, and a conviction in his mind that I would be assassinated if I remained.

Relying upon this promise of passports into Kentucky and of the protection of a military escort, I reported myself in person to General Crittenden before the twenty-four hours had expired, and was accompanied by Colonel Baxter. I there and then obtained from General Crittenden a renewal of his promise. This was on the 5th; and the morning of the 7th was agreed upon for me to start, and Captain Gillespie was designated as the man to put me through with his company of cavalry. Before that time arrived, I was arrested upon a warrant for treason, issued by Robert B. Reynolds, the Confederate Commissioner—a third-rate county-court lawyer, a drunken and corrupt *sot,* who had been kicked out of a grocery [i.e., saloon] a few days before by a mechanic, and who was afterwards taken up from the pavements of the street, in a beastly state of intoxication, by Rebel troops, and lodged in the guard-house! See a drawing of this beautiful specimen of a judge—a fit representative of the morality and integrity of the Confederate Government!

Here follows the warrant, issued upon the application and *false*

Robert B. Reynolds, the drunken Commissioner who committed Parson Brownlow to prison.

swearing of that *corrupt scoundrel* and most unprincipled knave, *J. Crozier Ramsey*, Confederate Attorney for the State of Tennessee:

> Confederate States of America,
> District of Tennessee

TO THE MARSHAL OF SAID DISTRICT:

J. C. Ramsey, Confederate States District Attorney for said district, having MADE OATH before me, that he is informed and believes that William G. Brownlow, a citizen of said district, and owing allegiance and fidelity to the Confederate States, but, being moved and seduced by the instigation of the devil, and not having the fear of God before his eyes, did wilfully, knowingly, and with malice aforethought, and feloniously, commit the crime of TREASON against the Confederate States, by then and there, within said district and *since the 10th day of June last*, publishing a weekly and tri-weekly paper, known as "Brownlow's Knoxville Whig," said paper had a large circulation in said district, and also circulated in the United States, and contained, weekly, divers of editorials written by the said Brownlow, which said editorials were treasonable against the Confederate States of America, and did then and there commit treason, and prompt others to commit treason, by speech as well as publication; did as aforesaid commit treason, and did give aid and comfort to the United States, both of said Governments being in a state of war with each other. You are therefore commanded to arrest the said Brownlow, and bring him before me, to be dealt with as the law directs.

> R. B. REYNOLDS,
> *Commissioner, &c.*

J. C. RAMSEY,
C.S. Dist. Att'y
December 6, 1861

I was arrested by the marshal, refused a trial, and refused bail, though my friends voluntarily offered a bond of ONE HUNDRED THOUSAND DOLLARS. While in the hands of the marshal, I addressed the following note to General Crittenden, and sent it by Colonel Williams:

> Knoxville, Dec. 6, 1861

MAJOR-GENERAL CRITTENDEN:

I am now under an arrest, upon a warrant issued by Commissioner Reynolds, at the instance of J. Crozier Ramsey, upon a charge of treason, founded upon sundry articles published in the Knoxville Whig since the 10th of June last.

I am here, as you will recollect, upon your invitation and the instructions of your Secretary of War to give me passports into the old Government. Claiming your protection, as I do, I shall await your early response.

Very respectfully, &c.,

W. G. BROWNLOW

No response was made to this note until the next day, and I was cast into prison. This gross breach of faith, both by the War Department at Richmond and the general in command at Knoxville, is a disgrace to the Confederate Government—if such a Government, originating as it did in fraud, falsehood, and perjury, can be disgraced!

The next day I received from a self-conceited member of General Crittenden's staff—a fellow late from California—the following note. After receiving this note, I gave up the chase, and felt that the whole concern, civil and military, were alike unreliable, having no regard for their pledges:

Knoxville, Dec. 7, 1861

W. G. BROWNLOW:

SIR: Your note, stating that you were under an arrest upon a warrant upon a charge of treason, &c., has been handed to General Crittenden.

He desires me to say, in reply, that in view of all of the facts of the case (which need not be recapitulated here, for you are familiar with them), HE DOES NOT CONSIDER THAT YOU ARE HERE UPON HIS INVITATION IN SUCH MANNER AS TO CLAIM HIS PROTECTION FROM AN INVESTIGATION BY THE CIVIL AUTHORITIES OF THE CHARGES AGAINST YOU, which he clearly understood from yourself and your friends you would not seek to avoid.

Respectfully, yours, &c.,

HARRY I. THORNTON,
A.D.C.

This corrupt man Ramsey, after issuing this warrant, accompanied it with a part of one of the editorials he had falsely sworn was issued since the 10th of June, 1861, at which time the State voted out.[3] . . . [A]lthough he swore in his warrant, and published the falsehood in the paper, that the article appeared since the 10th of June, the truth is it appeared on the 25th of May, and *before* the State voted out! One of

3. The actual date of the referendum that formalized the state's secession was June 8.

the reasons why he refused me a trial was that he knew I would produce a file of my papers and convict him of *false swearing*. . . .

This man Ramsey, in swearing a lie with a view to injure me, was
influenced by his deep-seated malice. He is the son of the vain old *historian of Tennessee*,[4] against whom I brought and sustained a suit for a
nefarious *bank-swindle*, and to avoid the damages of which, the old
rebel has put his property out of his hands, making this corrupt son the
trustee!

Besides, this Attorney for the Commonwealth of the Confederacy
attempted to get up a company of volunteers, but never was able to
muster more than *thirty* men; and, being detected in drawing rations
and clothing for sixty-five, he was, under General Zollicoffer's reign at
Knoxville, drummed out of the service. Let the reader turn to the
drawing of this man, and look at his hang-dog countenance as he "re-
tires" to the tune of the Rogues' March!

Being refused a trial and refused bail, as good and as strong as East
Tennessee could afford, I was confined in the common jail of the
county. And for what? For *treason* growing out of newspaper editorials! The warrant sued out by this judicial functionary contains within
itself no charge of treason, though he afterwards brought out a garbled
extract from the foregoing editorials, and alleged that therein lay the
treason. Every man of legal knowledge will see that the publication of
a newspaper, however objectionable its matter may be, does not
amount to treason. The object of this hardened villain, and the numerous cowardly scoundrels associated with him, was to subject me to
close confinement in a crowded and most uncomfortable jail. In this
these vile conspirators succeeded; but the reader will agree, after pe-
rusing these pages, that they have made but little by the operation.
And when the whole affair is done with, they will have made still less.

I became satisfied, after I went into jail and had slips of newspapers
conveyed to me, that General Carroll had not acted in good faith
towards me. . . .

The only apology I can offer for Carroll in his deceptive course is

4. James G. M. Ramsey—the father of Brownlow's nemesis, J. Crozier Ramsey—
was the author of *Annals of Tennessee to the End of the Eighteenth Century* . . . (Charleston, 1853).

that of his habits of drunkenness, his villainous associates in Knoxville, and the fact that he occupied as his quarters the house of the most unmitigated scoundrel in Knoxville, *John Hooper Crozier*—a man whose baseness and villainies I have held up to public gaze for years. Such cowards and malicious rascals as this surrounded Carroll, took possession of him, drenched him in liquor, and used him to do their dirty work!

But I was thrown into this jail, a drawing of which is herewith submitted, where I found *about one hundred and fifty* Union men, old and young, representing all professions. The jail was so crowded that on the lower floor we had not room for all to lie down at one time. The prisoners took rest by turns, a portion standing while the others slept. There was not a chair, bench, stool, block, table, or any other article of furniture, in the building, save a dirty wooden bucket and a tin cup, used for watering the occupants of the room. A bucketful would not go round, as the weather was at times warm and many of the prisoners were feverish. To supply them with water, a hogshead was placed by the side of the jail, and a boy with a cart hauled water through the day. One prisoner at a time was allowed to go out with the bucket and draw it full, under an escort of bayonets. About twenty-four men were kept around the jail in arms, and on the inside at the windows, which were allowed to be up in daylight only to give us fresh air. Through the windows we could see these dirty, sweating, insulting, and abusive Rebel soldiers go to the hogshead and wash their hands and faces in it. I remonstrated, telling these ill-bred fellows that this water was our only dependence for drinking-water. The reply was, "By G——d, sir, we will have you know that where a Jeff Davis man washes his face and hands is good enough for any d——d Lincolnite to drink!" We, of course, had no remedy but to submit.

The food given the prisoners to eat was not fit for a good and trusty dog to devour. It was composed of the scraps and leavings of a dirty hotel kept by the jailer and deputy-marshal of the Confederacy—the meat and bread sometimes half raw, sometimes burned, and always a scanty supply. I never tasted a particle of it, but was allowed the privilege of having my meals sent from home three times each day, an officer examining my basket as it came in and went out, to see that there was no correspondence between me and the Unionists out-of-doors. As this vile treatment and loathsome food produced disease, and, added to colds, often fell upon the bowels, the Rebel brutes who guarded us were furnished with additional opportunities for offering us personal indignity.

Blackguard songs were sung for our benefit, and we were all cursed and denounced both day and night. In marching us out and into the prison, we were ordered to "walk faster," and threatened with the bayonet if we did not obey. The most insulting of these sentinels were those from the Cotton States, men heralded to the world as the "flower of the Southern youth" and the "best blood" of the Confederacy.

There was one gentleman who visited us either daily or every other day: he was a gentleman and a humane man. I allude to Dr. Gray, Brigade Surgeon. He did all he could to prevent this sort of treatment, and had some benches made for the prisoners to sit on, and a sort of table upon which to place their scanty meals. But the feeling was, as a general thing, that any sort of treatment and fare were "too good for a set of d——d Union-shriekers and bridge-burners," as they styled all the prisoners.

Here my jail-journal commences, written in prison, with a lead-pencil, in small blank-books I kept in my side pocket. I will give it, without any polish or the slightest improvement, just as it was sketched— written amidst the crowd and clamor of so many men, some sick, others impatient and tired, but all respectful to me and kind to each other.

Friday (sunset), Dec. 6 [1861]—I was committed to the jail of Knox county this evening upon a warrant sued out by the Confederate Attorney, *J. C. Ramsey*, upon a false oath he swore before a drunken commissioner, *Reynolds*, charging me with treason in the editorials of my paper. The only editorial cited was written in May, before Tennessee separated from the Federal Government.

I have found many old acquaintances here and long-tried friends; and whilst some were glad to see me in no worse condition, and in expectation of hearing the current news of the day, as well as from their families, others shed tears upon taking me by the hand, grasping it in

Parson Brownlow entering the Knoxville Jail.

silence. As a general thing, I have found them down in spirits and expecting the worst results. Some of them have been here since October,
some since November, and others were committed but recently.

Some of them have said to me that they "never expected to come to
this"—that they had "never before looked through the grates of a jail."
I have cheered them up as far as I have been able to do. Having them
around me, I addressed them in this language:

> Gentlemen, don't take your confinement so much to heart. Rather glory in
> it, as patriots, devoted to your country and to your principles. What are you
> here for? Not for stealing; not for counterfeiting; not for murder; but for your
> devotion to the Stars and Stripes, the glorious old banner under which Wash-
> ington conquered, lived, and died. You will yet enjoy your liberties, and be
> permitted to die beneath the folds of the old Star-Spangled Banner, the sacred
> emblem of a common nationality. The Federal Government will crush out
> this wicked rebellion and liberate us, if we are not brutally murdered; and if
> we are, we die in a good cause. I am here with you to share your sorrows and
> sufferings, and here I intend to stay until the Rebels release me or execute me,
> or until the Federal army shall come to my rescue. You may take a different
> view of the subject, but I regard this as the proudest day of my life.

Saturday, Dec. 7—This morning, *forty* of our number, under a heavy
military escort, were sent off to Tuscaloosa. Thirty-one others arrived
to take their places, from Cocke, Greene, and Jefferson counties. They
bring us tales of woe from their respective counties, as to the treatment
of Union men and Union families by the drunken and debauched cavalry in this rebellion. They are taking all the fine horses they can find,
and appropriating them to their own use; they are entering houses,
breaking open drawers and chests, seizing money, blankets, and whatever they can use.

The dirty organ of the mob who have placed me here—the Knoxville *Register*—has opened upon me; and, now that I have no paper in
which to reply, shut up in solitary confinement, it will keep up a regular fire upon me. . . .

Sunday, Dec. 8—Three others arrived from Cocke county, telling us
tales of horror as to the treatment of Union men by the ruffian troops
of Jeff Davis. Self-styled Vigilance Committees are prowling over the

country like wolves, and military mobs, armed to the teeth, are arresting men upon suspicion of hostility to their new Government, and shooting others down in the field. They speak of the case of poor *Pearce*, a quiet man, a Methodist class-leader, shot down in his own field with a musket-ball—not for any offence he had ever committed, but simply for being a Union man. I knew him personally, and know him to have been a harmless man. A brother of this villainous attorney, Ramsey, was in the crowd that murdered Pearce.

Monday, Dec. 9—More prisoners arrived this evening. Twenty-eight are in from Jefferson and Cocke counties. Some of the Jefferson county prisoners have given us the particulars of the hanging of [Jacob M.] Hensie [actually Henshaw] and [Henry] Fry [for bridge-burning] upon the same limb of an oak-tree over or close by the railroad-track. The bloody scoundrel who tied the knot was one Colonel [Danville] Leadbetter, a native of Maine, who, after serving fifteen years in the United States army, married a gang of negroes at Mobile, and has become the great champion of Southern Rights. He ordered these two men to hang four days and nights, and the trains to pass by them slowly, so that the passengers could see, and kick, and strike with canes their dead bodies, from the front and rear platforms of the cars, as they passed—which was actually done. I shall illustrate the scene with an engraving if I ever live to get out of this prison. And I propose, if ever the Federal army shall capture East Tennessee—as I believe it will—and with it this murderer, *Leadbetter*, that he shall hang on the same limb, and that Fry's widow shall tie the knot around his infernal neck.

Tuesday, Dec. 10—The tedium of prison-life has rather oppressed us all to-day. It has been relieved a little by our coming in contact with some insolent Southern negroes. One in uniform, from Alabama, has been guarding us with a double-barrelled shot-gun, and has been insulting and abusive. Another negro came into the jail and threw slugs of lead through the grates into the iron cage of one of our prisoners. We have all to submit to this sort of treatment. When we are put here, we are deprived of our weapons, pocket-knives, and money, and all are confiscated, leaving us helpless. Some of our men had several hundred dollars in their pockets, and all had more or less money.

Hanging of Fry and Hensie near the railroad, by Colonel Leadbetter.

One of the scoundrels who took an active part in having me put here is *Colonel W. M. Churchwell*, the great bank-swindler, whose dishonesty I brought to light in a suit in chancery, all of which is now on record. One of the privates in Churchwell's regiment, by the name of *Barker*, is now here a prisoner for having knocked down his captain. Barker was run against Churchwell for colonel, and actually beat him one hundred and eighty votes; but Carroll gave the certificate in favor of Churchwell. Churchwell afterwards had Barker chained to a tree, and more recently he had Captain Jackson arrested for heading a petition to C. to resign on the score of *incompetency*.

Wednesday, Dec. 11—C. A. Haun, a man about twenty-seven years of age, was taken out to-day and hung, on a charge of bridge-burning. He had but a short notice of his sentence, having been condemned without any defence allowed him by a drum-head and whiskey-drinking court-martial. I think that he was notified of his coming death about one hour in advance. I know he desired a Methodist preacher sent for to sing and pray with him, and this was refused him: so that he was forced to exchange worlds without the "benefit of clergy." They drove up a cart with a coffin in it, surrounded by a hardened set of Rebel troops, displaying their bayonets and looking and talking savagely. It is stated to us that one of the Rebel chaplains officiated at the hanging, and stated that Haun desired him to say that he had been misled by the Union leaders and papers and was sorry for his conduct, whereupon Haun contradicted him, and said that he had admitted no such thing. Haun leaves a young wife and two or three little children. I had, myself, sooner be Haun than any one of his murderers.

Fifteen more prisoners came in to-day from Greene and Hancock counties, charged with having been armed as Union men and accustomed to drill, which I have no doubt is true. What their fate will be, God only knows. These savage beasts of the Southern Confederacy are prepared to hang a man for saying that Secession is wrong or unconstitutional, although John C. Calhoun admitted this much himself.

Thursday, Dec. 12—Fifteen of our prisoners were started to Tuscaloosa this morning, to remain there as prisoners of war. They had no

C. A. Haun parting from his Family before his Execution.

trial, but were sent upon their admission that they had been found in arms, as Union men, preparing to defend themselves against the murderous assaults and highway-robberies daily committed by the so-called Confederate cavalry. Poor fellows! They hated to go; and no wonder, for they are treated like dogs on the way, as well as after they get there!

Friday, Dec. 13—Three more prisoners in to-day, from Hancock and Hawkins counties. Charge, as usual, Union men, attached to a company of Home-Guards. . . .

Saturday, Dec. 14—Three more prisoners from the upper counties were brought in to-day. They speak of the outrages perpetrated by these Rebel troops, and of their murderous spirit. Three officers visited me today. Lieutenant-Colonel [E. J.] Golladay stated to me that, whilst he was not informed as to what they would do with me, he was in favor of sending me to Nashville,[5] boarding me at a hotel, giving me the privileges of the city until the war was over, but confining me to its limits. I told him that his mode of punishment was not severe, but that I preferred his Government should carry out its stipulations with me and send me beyond their limits.

General Carroll visited me, but was, as I supposed, more drunk than usual. He thought that I ought to be out of this, but that I ought to be willing to swear allegiance to the Confederate Government. I told him that I would lie here until I died with old age before I would take such an oath. I did not consider that he had a Government; I regarded it as a big Southern mob. It had never been recognized by any Government on earth, and never would be!

Sunday, Dec. 15—Started thirty-five of our lot to Tuscaloosa, to be held during the war. Levi Trewhitt, an able lawyer, but an old man, will never get back. His sons came up to see him, but were refused the privilege. Dr. [William] Hunt, from the same county of Bradley, has also gone. His wife came sixty miles to see him, and came to the jail-door, but was refused admittance. Dr. Hunt's offence is twofold. First,

5. Nashville was still in Confederate hands at this time.

his wife is my wife's only sister; and, next, he holds the clerkship of the Chancery Court, and *Tom Campbell*, the judge-advocate on the court-martial, has a brother-in-law whom he desires to put in the office. I have told the doctor that as soon as his office could be declared vacant he would be turned out, and McMillan, the brother-in-law of Campbell, put in his place. . . .

Monday, Dec. 16—Brought in Dr. Wells and Colonel Morris, of Knox county, two clever men and good citizens. Their offence is that they are Union men, first; and, next, as old Whigs, they voted and electioneered against this scoundrel Ramsey, the Confederate Attorney, when he was beaten for the United States Congress, about two years ago. He now has a chance of paying these gentlemen back!

I have this day mailed the following letter to the Secretary of War at Richmond:

Knoxville Jail, Dec. 16, 1861

Hon. J. P. Benjamin:

You authorized General Crittenden to give me passports and an escort to send me into the old Government, and he invited me here for that purpose; but a third-rate county-court lawyer, acting as your Confederate attorney, took me out of his hands and cast me into this prison. I am anxious to learn which is your highest authority—the Secretary of War, a major-general, or a dirty little drunken attorney such as *J. C. Ramsey* is!

You are reported to have said to a gentleman in Richmond that I am a bad man, dangerous to the Confederacy, and that you desire me out of it. Just give me my passports, and I will do for your Confederacy more than the devil has ever done—I will quit the country!

I am, &c.,

W. G. Brownlow

Tuesday, Dec. 17—Brought in a Union man from Campbell county to-day, leaving behind six small children, and their mother dead. This man's offence is holding out for the Union!

Two more carts drove up with coffins in them and a heavy military guard around them. This produced in our circle of prisoners great consternation, for we did not know certainly who were to hang. They, however, came into the jail and marched out Jacob Harmon and his son Henry, and hung them up on the same gallows! The old man was a man of property, quite old and infirm, and they compelled him to sit on the scaffold and see his son, a young man, hang first; then he was ordered up and hung by his side. They were charged with bridge-burning, but protested to the last that they were not guilty. I know not how this was; but the laws of Tennessee only send a man to the penitentiary for such offences.

To-night, two brothers—named Walker—came in from Hawkins county, charged with having "*talked Union talk.*"

Wednesday, Dec. 18—Discharged sixty prisoners to-day, who had been in prison from three to five weeks—taken through mistake, as was said, there being nothing against them. Business suffering at home, unlawfully seized upon and thrust into this uncomfortable jail, they are now turned out by the corrupt, wicked, God-defying, and hell-deserving authorities of this usurped, bogus, and truly infamous Confederacy. We are getting our number reduced, but these devils will replenish our prison as long as they can find Union men in East Tennessee; and that will be until they kill them all off!

Thursday, Dec. 19—I have now only been fourteen days in this *Union Hall*, but I am feeling the effects of the cold nights and confinement. My old disease, *bronchitis*, is troubling me. So well am I satisfied of the inflammation of the bronchi, or ramifications of the windpipe, that I have called in a physician and had him insert a silk cord in my breast just below the chin, so as to bring the inflammation to the surface.

To-night twelve more Union prisoners were brought in from lower East Tennessee, charged with belonging to Colonel Clift's regiment of Union men, arming and drilling to go over to Kentucky and join the Federal army.

Friday, Dec. 20—General Carroll, hearing of my indisposition, came in to-day and offered to remove me to their dirty hospital. I declined the offer—did not want passports to where I would likely be poisoned in twenty-four hours. I told him I was ready to receive passports to go beyond the limits of the Confederacy. If these could not be had, I de-

Execution of Jacob Harmon and his son Henry.

sired to remain where I was. This is a terrible night! The sentinels are all drunk—howling like wolves—rushing to our windows with the ferocity of the Sepoys of India, and daring prisoners to show their heads—cocking their guns and firing off three of them into the jail, and pretending it was accidental. Merciful God! how long are we to be treated after this fashion?

Saturday, Dec. 21—Took out five of the prisoners brought here from the Clift expedition—liberated them by their agreeing to go into the Rebel army. Their dread of Tuscaloosa induced them to go into the service. They have offered this chance to all, and only sent off those who stubbornly refused.

The troops in town are on a general spree, for as many as twenty-five of them have been thrust into prison with us. I suspect they are made drunk and put into jail to get up a row with the Union prisoners. They are yelling all night like savages—some cursing Lincoln and the Union men, some cursing Davis and his Confederacy, and all swearing that they are sick of the war. I write this at midnight. . . .

Sunday, Dec. 22—Brought in old man Wamplar, an old Dutchman seventy years of age, from Greene county, charged with being an *Andy Johnson man*, and "talking Union talk." Sentinels are stationed in our rooms to watch us—cursing us all for d——d thieves, Tories, and scoundrels, to even guard whom is a disgrace, they allege. One of them carried the matter so far that one of our prisoners, *Tucker*, pitched into him and flogged him without arms, and in defiance of his musket.

Monday, Dec. 23—Officer of the day in charge of the sentinels furnished liquor to a portion of the prisoners, such as came out of the ranks of Secession. They got drunk. A general row was threatened. Union prisoners and Rebel sentinels played cards, and the former won the money.

Tuesday, Dec. 24—[Moses] White's regiment, some of whom have been guarding us, left to-day for Kentucky to join Zollicoffer's army. Many of them seemed to regret it—told our prisoners that they felt like [they were] going to their graves. Officer of the day came into the

jail and demanded all the cards. They were handed over to him, and
he burned them. We have but three men who play cards. To-night
they brought in one of their "Texas Rangers," who had deserted from
Manassas [Virginia]. He looks but little like killing Yankees. Various
troops put in jail during the day for drunkenness.

Wednesday, Dec. 25—The Union ladies in and around Knoxville applied to General Carroll for leave to send in a Christmas dinner. He
granted leave, and stated that he regarded it as an act of humanity.
The supply was abundant and sumptuous, and was most thankfully
received.

It affords me great pleasure to know that I have been able, out of my
basket of provisions and coffee-pot, to furnish several very old men,
and very sick, who could not eat what comes from the greasy inn. Two
of them are Baptist ministers, Messrs. Pope and Cate, each as much as,
or more than, *seventy* years of age. The first-named was sent here for
praying, in his pulpit, for the President of the United States. The latter
is here for cheering the Stars and Stripes as the banner neared his
house, borne by some men on horseback.

Thursday, Dec. 26—Some twelve Confederate troops, beastly drunk,
have to-day been confined in our jail for outraging all the decencies of
life. They make our jail a hell on earth. What an affliction it is to be
cursed with confinement in such a place and with such brutes as these
are! I am sick, without an appetite, and I fear I am taking the fever.
Several of our men are now sick, stretched out upon the floor; and
some of them, I have reason to believe, will never survive this confinement.

Friday, Dec. 27—Harrison Self, an industrious, honest, and heretofore peaceable man, a citizen of Greene county, was notified this
morning that he was to be hanged at four o'clock P.M. His daughter, a
noble girl, modest, and neatly attired, came in this morning to see him.
Heart-broken and bowed down under a fearful weight of sorrow, she
entered his iron cage, and they embraced each other most affection-
ately. My God, what a sight! What an affecting scene! May these eyes
of mine, bathed in tears, never look upon the like again! The weeping

Interview of W. H. H. Self with his daughter in Knoxville Jail.

of prisoners who beheld this scene brings to my mind the verses I sub-
join:

> Did Christ o'er sinners weep?
> And shall our cheeks be dry?
> Let floods of penitential grief
> Burst forth from every eye.
>
> The Son of God in tears,
> Angels with wonder see!
> Be thou astonished, O my soul:
> He shed those tears for thee.

But her short limit to remain with her father expired, and she came
out weeping bitterly, and shedding burning tears. Requesting me to
write a dispatch for her and sign her name to it, I took out my pencil
and a slip of paper, and wrote the following:

Knoxville, Dec. 27, 1861

Hon. JEFFERSON DAVIS:

My father, Harrison Self, is sentenced to hang at four o'clock this evening,
on a charge of bridge-burning. As he remains my earthly all, and all my hopes
of happiness centre in him, I implore you to pardon him.

ELIZABETH SELF

With this dispatch the poor girl hurried off to the office, some two
or three hundred yards from the jail; and about two o'clock in the af-
ternoon the answer came to General Carroll, telling him not to allow
Self to be hung. Self was turned out of the cage into the jail with the
rest of us, and looks as if he had gone through a long spell of sickness.
But what a thrill of joy ran through the heart of that noble girl! Self is
to be confined, as I understand, during the war. This is hard upon an
innocent man; but it is preferable to hanging.

Self stated that when he expected to hang, and only a few hours before Davis's dispatch came, the marshal and jailer, Fox, told him that
he was authorized to say to him that if he would confess his guilt as a
bridge-burner, under the gallows, and would state that BROWNLOW,

TRIGG, BAXTER, and TEMPLE[6] had put him up to it and furnished money to burn the bridges, he would be reprieved! He replied to the wicked, malicious, and infernal offer that he could not say so, as it would not be true. What an effort to involve innocent men! And what a temptation to the man about to hang! The men who authorized this bribe deserve the lowest and hottest apartments in the infernal regions.

Upon the jail-floor, in one corner, lies Madison Cate, low with fever, and upon a bit of old carpeting, with some sort of bundle under his aching head to serve as a pillow. I feel confident that he will die. Poor fellow! He is an honest man—a man who stays at home and attends to his own business. He has a little farm in Sevier county, a wife and six small and helpless children, and is here for being a Union man and mustering with a company of Union Guards. This is the head and front of his offending.

We have all just witnessed a thrilling scene. The wife of poor Cate came and presented herself in front of the jail, neatly attired, with an infant at her breast, of five or six weeks old—born, I think, since her husband's confinement! She asked leave to see her dying husband, but was refused at the door, by some one claiming to act upon authority. I put my head out of the window and remonstrated, telling them that it was a sin and a shame to refuse this poor woman, after coming so far, the liberty of seeing her husband, and seeing him for the last time! They allowed her to enter, but limited her stay to twenty minutes. She came in. And, oh, my soul! what a scene! Seeing the emaciated form of her husband on the floor, pining with sorrow and severe affliction, and destitute of every comfort, she approached with faltering step, and sank down upon his heaving breast, bathed in tears of anguish. I asked her to give me the babe as she ventured up; for I saw that she was unconscious of having it in her arms. In that condition, without a word, they remained until her twenty minutes expired, of which being noti-

6. Oliver P. Temple and Connally F. Trigg were Knoxville lawyers and leading Unionists. John Baxter, previously mentioned by Brownlow, was likewise a Knoxville lawyer. Originally a Unionist, Baxter embraced secession in August 1861. His late conversion, moderate stance, and continued friendship with Brownlow apparently made him suspect in the eyes of some secessionists.

Interview of Madison Cate with his Family.

fied, she rose up and retired. I hope I may never look upon such a scene again. Oh, what oppression! And yet this is the *spirit* of Secession! I find some consolation in the following verses:

> Oppression shall not always reign:
> There dawns a brighter day,
> When freedom, burst from every chain,
> Shall have triumphant sway.
>
> Then right shall over might prevail,
> And truth, like hero armed in mail,
> The hosts of tyrant wrong assail,
> And hold eternal sway![7]

The outside pressure against me I knew was very great, and the clamor for my blood, or rather for my *neck*, was to be heard among the Secession citizens on the street, and among the infuriated troops in camp and in the liquor-shops of the town. I really supposed, at one time, that they would hang me, and I made up my mind to meet the occasion like a man. In view of this fate, I sketched off a brief speech, which I intended to ask the privilege of delivering on the scaffold. I think they would have granted the request, from an intense curiosity to hear what I had to say in such a trying moment; and I believe I could have stood forth and said it in the face of ten thousand people. I give the speech just as I prepared it in pencil-writing, at intervals, in prison. I began writing it when they commenced hanging our prisoners:

Intended Speech under the Gallows

Fellow-Countrymen: I have often addressed many of you, upon different topics, but never under circumstances like those which now surround me, as I feel that I am speaking for the last time. I suppose I have been sentenced to hang by a court-martial sitting in this city: I say I *suppose* so, for I have never had any trial, or even a notice of a trial being in progress. So it has been with those who have been executed before me. It is alike a matter of indifference

---

7. Here Brownlow interrupted his jail diary to insert the commentary and speech that follow. The diary resumes with the January 1, 1862, entry.

whether I was tried by *that* court-martial in my absence and in the absence of witnesses and counsel, or whether I had been present; the result would have been death. The judge advocate, THOMAS J. CAMPBELL, is a perfidious man, as destitute of real honor and purity of purpose as he is of true courage and manly virtue. Associated with him is JAMES D. THOMAS, a man who was expelled from the Methodist ministry for whipping his wife and slandering his venerable old father-in-law! This man Thomas has advocated on the bench, in open court-martial, the sending of the Union masses of East Tennessee to Alabama and Mississippi, and working them in the field, under negro overseers, and the hanging of the Union leaders here! Justice at the hands of such a set of men is the last thing I would expect. Indeed, there is more glory in being put to death by such men than in being acquitted, after going through the forms of a trial.

It is known to many of you that I had left home to avoid personal violence, and was out of the reach of the mob, who could not find me, after repeated efforts by squads sent out, armed, by that arch-hypocrite and would-be murderer, W. B. Wood, of Alabama. In my concealment I was informed by a letter from Major-General Crittenden, in command at this place, that he was instructed by the Secretary of War at Richmond, Mr. Benjamin, to give me passports and a military escort to conduct me out of this bogus Government into the Federal Government; and I was invited to appear at his head-quarters in twenty-four hours, where he promised me that I should be furnished with said passports. I was there within the time specified, accompanied by Colonel Baxter, the arrangement was made, and the company of Captain Gillespie designated as my escort. But that evening, just before sundown, I was arrested upon a warrant issued by that disgraceful specimen of our nature, *Commissioner Reynolds*, upon the false oath of *Attorney Ramsey*, a corrupt man, for whom no decent Secessionist entertains any respect. The charge against me was *treason*, founded upon editorials, one of which has been published, in part, by Ramsey, in the Knoxville *Register*; and although the miserable man swore that the editorial was published *since the 10th of June*, at which time the State voted out, my files will show that it was published on the 25th of May.

Thus I was taken out of the hands of a major-general and of his Secretary of War by a worthless little Confederate lawyer, and thrown into the common jail of this county; refused bail, when the best the county affords was offered; and, up to this eventful hour, I have been denied a trial, and an opportunity to defend myself before the court condemning me to an ignominious death. The proof of all that is here charged will be found in the correspondence cited, which I have placed in the hands of a friend for publication. It will show that these parties, one and all, have acted a treacherous part towards me, and have violated their pledges and faith. Their perfidy and treachery are absolutely disgraceful to their bogus Government, if indeed such a Government can be disgraced.

Some hostile reminiscences of the past, as between other cowardly, mean, and murderous men of this city and myself, will appear in the documents I leave behind; and I request my sons to publish them, even at the cost of their lives. I desire to bear my testimony, even in a dying hour, to the perfidy, double-dealing, and cowardly course toward me of that prince of hypocrites and great embodiment of human deceit, Campbell Wallace, the president of the railroad, and one of the great lights of Secession. I warn all men present, and all who may hear of this statement, never to confide in that man. He is supremely selfish, notoriously insincere, and would sell his interest in his God—which, I fear, is not a very large one—for money!

I must also bear witness to the treachery and insincerity of William G. McAdoo, who, while meeting me with a smile and professing friendship, stated to John Black that I ought to be kept in prison during this war. This man was on the verge of starvation, and without credit, when I took it upon myself to attend the sitting of our Legislature, some years ago, and help make him District Attorney. He since lost one wife and married a second owning a gang of negroes and a rice-plantation in Georgia, and has turned over to Secession. I warn my family and friends never to confide in him.

Fellow-countrymen, I am shortly to be executed—not for any crime punishable with death, but for my devotion to my country, her laws and Constitution. I die for refusing to espouse the cause of this wicked rebellion; and I glory in it, strange as you may think it. I could have lived, if I had taken an oath of allegiance to this so-called Confederacy. Rather than stultify myself and disgrace my family by such an oath, I agree to die! I never could sanction this Government, and I trust that no child of mine will ever do it. Look at the past history of the leaders and originators of this rebellion. There is not a man of unstained character to be found among them. Yancey is a convicted murderer, who killed his uncle (Dr. Earl, of South Carolina), and, instead of going to England [as a Confederate commissioner] to intrigue against this Government, he would have been in prison had he not been pardoned by the Governor of that State. [Louis T.] Wigfall, a Confederate Senator and a general, fled from his native State of South Carolina to Texas to escape the horrors of assassination, became a collecting attorney for large amounts, and then swindled his employers out of their dues, murdering as many as two men in Texas. [John B.] Floyd, while Governor of my native State, was guilty of swindling the State out of some thirty thousand dollars of the Washington Monument Fund intrusted to his care; while in Buchanan's Cabinet, in violation of his oath, he stole, besides large amounts of bonds, the guns, forts, and ammunition of the Federal Government, to aid in carrying on this infamous rebellion. [John] Slidell, another intriguer, who never had an honest emotion of soul in his life, assisted, while in the United States Senate, to pass through Congress that great swindle of the age, the *"Houmans Land Grant"*—a swindle so gigantic and a cheat so enormous that the next Congress revoked the grant. Benjamin, your Secretary of War, and one of the men engaged in deceiving me, was expelled from a New England college for stealing money and jewelry out of the trunks of his fellow-students: he afterwards got into the Senate from Louisiana by turning from a Whig to a Democrat, and became the partner of Slidell in the Houmans swindle. [Jacob] Thompson, the Mississippi member of Buchanan's Cabinet, while Secretary of the Interior, was a partner in stealing some Indian Trust Bonds, and, when about to be dismissed for the offence, fled from the Federal capital by night, to avoid a prosecution. [Howell] Cobb, the Georgia member of Buchanan's Cabinet, speculated in stocks, using Government money, and was detected in it; and all this was at a time when he was acting under oath, as the head of the Treasury Department. Davis, your President, after his State had borrowed millions, led the way in the work of repudiation and in defrauding Mississippi's honest creditors. [Robert A.] Toombs, the big man of your Government at Richmond, was the confederate of [South Carolina congressmen Lawrence M.] Keitt and [Preston S.] Brooks in their attempt to assassinate [Massachusetts senator Charles] Sumner [by caning, in 1856]. [William G.] Swan, your Congressman from this district, and an original Secessionist, is the forger of the [Andrew] Johnson letters to [Massachusetts philanthropist Amos] Lawrence, with a view to swindle the latter out of ten thousand dollars [by claiming the money would be used to aid East Tennessee Unionists]. These, and a host of others like them, are the men who originated and are carrying on this Southern Rebellion. Ought not any honest man to prefer to hang rather than act with *such* men in a wicked crusade against the mild sway of the best Government on earth?

But I must close. Solemn thought! I die, with confidence that the United States Government will crush out this rebellion during the coming spring and summer. Mark my prediction! I would like to be living when that is done; but I must resign myself to my fate.

I have a word to say as it regards my family. I leave a wife and seven children to the mercies of a cold-hearted world. I hope the Union men of the country will be kind to them, and seek to impress their minds with what is true—that they are not disgraced, but honored, by my death. Let me be shrouded in the sacred folds of the Star-Spangled Banner; and let my children's children know that the last words I uttered on earth were,

> Forever float that standard sheet!
> Where breathes the foe but falls before us,
> With Freedom's soil beneath our feet,
> And Freedom's banner streaming o'er us!

January 1, 1862—For the last four or five days I have been very sick, and I am now *salivated* from an excess of mercury. I have, therefore, not made any note of what has passed. Captain [George H.] Monsarrat, late of Nashville, is in charge of this post at present; and I will do him the justice to say that he has treated me and my family with great kindness, and as I would expect to be treated by a gentleman. Upon the testimony of Dr. [O. F.] Hill, one of my family physicians, Captain Monsarrat has had me brought to a private room, on my own lot, and guarded as at the jail. . . .

Upon learning that I was about to be removed, and upon getting a letter from the War Department to the effect that I ought not to have been imprisoned, the miscreant Ramsey went into court and ordered my release upon the civil arrest; but an officer of the army, who accompanied the notice of my release to my bedside, re-arrested me under the military authority, and placed an armed guard at my door. . . .

Jan. 28, 1862—For days and nights I have been very sick, and have ceased to keep up my regular journal. A strong guard has been kept around my house, and my friends and neighbors have been denied the privilege of visiting me. That prince of villains, tyrants, and murderers, *Colonel Leadbetter*, has come rushing into my room, and insultingly demanded to know when I would be ready to *leave the Confederacy*—adding that "very many persons were anxious that I should be sent out of the country." I replied to him that I was improving, but utterly unable to travel, as I could not sit up, but assured him that I would go as soon as I could travel, and that I was more anxious to leave than his "many persons" could be for me to go. He insultingly rose up, started out, and told me to let him know when I felt able to travel.

Jan. 30—One *Burch Cook*, the captain of a company, and the drunken tool of this Leadbetter, came in and read me an order requiring my instant removal to the hospital, where I could be guarded more effectually and be prevented from plotting treason with Union leaders. I protested against being dragged out of my room, when unable to sit up, and placed in a cold room without fire, to vacate a feather-bed and go upon such a mattress as I would find in the hospital. He spoke in an abrupt and insulting manner to my wife—as only a coarse, vulgar man, a profane swearer, and a common drunkard, such as he is, would do. He pretended to doubt the reality of my sickness, and said he was instructed to bring in one of the hospital-surgeons to examine me. Accordingly, Dr. Love was called in: he examined me thoroughly, and gave a certificate to Cook to the effect that my removal at that time to the place designated would jeopardize my life. This seemed to defeat their hellish schemes to get me out where they could poison me or have me assassinated, and they at once placed a *double guard* around me, with orders not to allow any one to enter the house but my family physician. Cook came in and directed that a sentinel should stand in each of the doors leading into my room, with a loaded musket, and also stationed guards around the house. This was the order of the scoundrel *Leadbetter*; and *Cook* was a suitable instrument to execute such an order.

Saturday, 8th February—Leadbetter this day refused James R. Cocke, one of my lawyers, the privilege of visiting me, although Cocke is one of the moderate but decided Secessionists of the town. He denounced me to Cocke, and insultingly told him that he had no business to visit such a man!

Sunday, 9th February—This day was celebrated, in part, by a gang of these Rebel troops congregating in my office and library, and in my back yard, playing cards and swearing. No remedy for a man in such cases! F. S. Heiskell, an old citizen of this county, and a friend of mine, made application to *Leadbetter* for leave to visit me, but was insultingly refused. He was told that I was a bad man, and that he ought not to contaminate himself by visiting me. Major Heiskell controverted the statement—told him that he had known me for years, and that he knew me to be a clever and an honorable man. Angry words were exchanged, and the parties separated.

Wednesday, 12th February—The Rebel mob seized upon the hall in East Knoxville—used in part as a Methodist church, where a Union congregation worships—and placed in it a portion of one of their regiments. The representatives of the congregation remonstrated, saying that it had been fitted out at considerable expense by a poor congregation of Methodists, mostly mechanics. Major Burleson replied that he had ordered it to be taken because he understood it was "the property of old Brownlow." The members told him that it was not—that Brownlow was indeed one of the largest contributors towards building it and fitting it up, but that it was conveyed to trustees for the threefold purposes of worship, education, and temperance. They told him that Brownlow held his membership there, and that but for him it never would have been built—but that he was not even one of its trustees.

This man was urged to destroy the hall by a hardened villain, *John H. Crozier*, whose nomination has just been rejected by the Legislature, in secret session, by an overwhelming vote. Governor Harris had nominated him as a commissioner to settle the war-claims. Only *one* East Tennessean voted to confirm his nomination. There is half a million of dollars involved in the settlement. Crozier is a scoundrel, and a brother of the man lately involved in swindling the State out of her bonds through some banking-operations.

Thursday, Feb. 14—The *Register*, the Secession organ, contains a call for a meeting of the citizens of the town and county to organize a regiment for home-defence, in view of the approach of the Federal army.[8]

8. Early in February 1862 Union Army and Navy forces under General Ulysses S. Grant invaded the state along the Tennessee River northwest of Nashville, capturing Fort Henry on February 6.

Procession formed and marched to the court-house, Confederate flag flying, and drum and fife in operation. Crozier and Sneed headed the procession—men who were never known to resent an insult, and whose families have packed up their goods to leave. These two men addressed the crowd, and they adjourned to meet again.

Friday, Feb. 15—War-meeting reassembled at the court-house. *Rev. Isaac Lewis* presided—an old Locofoco Secessionist, who has three grown sons, neither of whom can be induced to go into the service, but all are candidates for civil offices. Colonel Baxter made a speech, and killed off, very properly, their meeting; reviewed their treatment of Union men. Rev. Richard O. Curry, a Presbyterian, made a violent speech against Union men. Disgraceful assault upon Union men, and a slander against their patriotism!

I have this day written a letter to Colonel [Robert B.] Vance, complaining of my condition; but, as I concluded it, he called in to visit me, and I read him the contents, as follows:

At Home, Feb. 15, 1862

COLONEL ROBERT VANCE:

I am glad to learn that you are in command of this post, and I hope you may be continued while it is my lot to remain here under guard and in prison. As you are no doubt aware, I have not been able to write for several days; and this hasty letter I indite while propped up in bed. But I write to give you an account of my treatment by those associated with you and preceding you.

I think I may venture to say, by way of preliminary, that I am not prone to utter complaints, but usually exercise a good degree of patience. For the first five weeks of the last seven that a guard has been placed around and in my room, I have voluntarily given them three meals in each day, seating them at my table with my family, considering it no hardship, as I knew most of them to be Union men forced into the service. When even a different class of men were selected, who took possession of my library and office, where my two sons sleep—when, I say, this was seized upon and turned into a guard-house, rocking-chairs broken to pieces, carpet ruined, and books damaged—when my coal and wood were taken and consumed, though dear and difficult to procure—and when I have furnished their guard-house candles all the time, though none are to be had in the market—I have not complained. When your predecessor, *Colonel Leadbetter*, has refused my son John the privilege of collecting debts due me from the clerks and sheriffs of surrounding counties, which they are ready and anxious to pay me, and which, in my broken-down condition, I really need to live on, I have uttered no words of complaint. When, for several days past, out of a family of thirteen in number only my wife, my son John, and two negroes were off the sick-list—when both the *mumps* and *measles* were introduced by armed sentinels standing day and night in my room and at my doors—I have not uttered even a single word of complaint. When my house, and especially my passage and front portico, have been shamefully abused by these sentinels, disfigured with mud and tobacco, I have submitted in silence, though conscious of the bad treatment given me. When we have all been kept from sleep by the walking, talking, singing, and swearing, and by a change of these guards every two hours—when they have rudely rushed into my bedchamber, as they said, to get warm—I have submitted without one word of complaint. I have felt that there is a better day coming for me and my family, if I am not assassinated—which is threatened me on every hand! I have had, and I still have, confidence in the final success of the principles for which I am made to suffer these cruel indignities; and hence I have been silent.

But last night, when my wife attempted to close and fasten a back door by which my bedroom is entered, and it the only fastening to my room in the rear of the building, she was insultingly notified by the sentinel, a drunken Secessionist, that *it must stand open all night*, and that such were his orders from *Captain Cook*, to whose company he was attached: she told him that it could not, and should not, stand open—that there were three other sick persons in the room besides me, and one of them a little daughter with fever; and she accordingly closed it upon him, and locked it, expecting him to break it down.

Of this treatment, Colonel Vance, I do complain, and especially as threats are made that the door shall be kept open to-night. My appeal for relief is to you. To your predecessor, *Leadbetter*, I can make no appeal; for he never had a gentlemanly emotion of soul in his life; and, if he were capable of such feelings, he is the willing and malicious instrument of a villainous clique here, of most corrupt, vindictive, and despicable scoundrels, of whom *John H. Crozier*, *J. C. Ramsey*, and *W. G. Swan* are chief.

There is no call for this double guard around me. It is done to oppress me and my family. My wife and children are treated as prisoners; and all marketing is excluded from the house by a military order not to allow any persons to enter my door or yard. I hope, for the honor of the Southern character, that no other private family within the eleven Seceded States is subjected to such an ordeal. Certain I am that such tyranny and oppression, such outrages and insults, will never diminish my esteem for the old United States Government, or increase my respect for the Southern Confederacy.

Feeble as I am, I am ready and anxious to go beyond your lines, as it will relieve my family of this oppression. If I cannot be removed, in accordance with the pledge of your War Department, I am willing, nay, desirous, to go back to jail, if that will secure the repose of an afflicted, insulted, and outraged family.

I am, very truly, &c.,

W. G. BROWNLOW

Sunday, Feb. 16—Colonel Vance, as might have been expected of a gentleman of his known character, relieved my family of this great annoyance of a double guard, and stationed *two* sentinels there, to relieve each other during the day, with instructions to retire at night, so as to allow us to sleep in quiet. Cook's men left the same day for Cumberland Gap, where it is hoped the Secession portion of them will find employment.

Monday, Feb. 17—A Georgia regiment arrived here to-day from Pensacola, under command of Colonel Mangum. A portion of them got drunk; took the town; called in front of the court-house to mob Colonel Baxter; Circuit Court in session; Baxter appeared, told them he was the man they were hunting, denounced the scoundrels who set them on him, and pointed out young Crozier as a goggle-eyed little scoundrel who had tried to set them on him.

Squads of the Georgia *patriots* have passed my house at different times, surveyed my premises, and inquired how strong the guard was. Colonel Vance to-night has put an additional guard of ten men at my house, to prevent their attacks.

Secessionists have received the news of the fall of Fort Donelson,[9]

9. After taking Fort Henry, Grant's force turned eastward and besieged Fort Donelson on the Cumberland River, capturing it and its large garrison on February 16. With Nashville thus exposed, Governor Harris and other state officials abandoned the city and fled to Memphis, which became the temporary capital. Nashville was occupied by Union troops later in February, and Memphis in June. Knoxville and the rest of East Tennessee, however, remained in Confederate hands until the autumn of 1863.

but have kept it a profound secret, until the members of the Legislature have arrived and disclosed it. They are in great trouble.

Tuesday, Feb. 18—The news of the fall of Fort Donelson no sooner reached here than several of our most *intense* Southern patriots packed up and left for other quarters. W. H. Sneed, John H. Crozier, W. G. McAdoo, [Knoxville Postmaster] C. W. Charlton, and poor *little Graves*,[10] have fled to parts unknown, going mostly in the direction of the Cotton States. These men are all original Secessionists but McAdoo, and they were, less than a week ago, proposing to raise a regiment for home-defence, and proposing to die in the last ditch. It is said that most of these men were looking back, as they took to flight, to see if Lincoln's invaders were coming. Regiment after regiment of Georgia troops have been arriving; but this has only made it look more like a fight approaching. . . .

Like the "Fishing Creek" warriors, these men will run on until they reach the other side of sundown. When they fled from Zollicoffer's battle-ground, they came into Knoxville bare-headed and bare-footed, on mules and stolen horses; and, although they were one hundred and fifty miles from where they got so terribly basted, they were still looking back to see if the "Lincolnites" were after them. A portion of these *racers* were the cowardly scoundrels who used to groan about my house and flourish their pistols and knives, swearing what they would do with my flag. They have at length come up with the Stars and Stripes in more hateful proportions than they found them at my house. Some of them have got their rights in this drive.

These rebels used to swear with emphasis, and with varied intonations, that they intended to "die in the last ditch." I think they are in search of this ditch, and in a fair way to find it. This heroic phrase is traceable to that country of dikes and ditches, Holland. It is said that William of Orange, when hard pressed by England and France, said that he would avoid beholding the ruin of his country by dying in the last ditch. His idea was to resist the invaders to the verge of the ocean,

10. Nowhere in Brownlow's book is "little Graves" identified. Possibly he was a son of J. R. Graves of Nashville, a secessionist and longtime religious adversary of the Parson.

and there yield up his life. These Southern rebels are looking out for that huge ditch, the Mississippi River. If they cross that—which I predict—they will have no ditch left them to die in except the Gulf of Mexico, where I hope they will all drown, as did the swine in the Sea of Galilee when the devils entered into them.

Stronghold after stronghold of these rebels is being carried by the Federals, and they are refusing to die in the last ditch. They afford us other exhibitions, such as helter-skelter, pell-mell, harum-scarum, hurry-skurry, skadaddle-skadiddle, devil-take-the-hindmost-man in fleeing from the *first* ditch. But the *last* ditch of the whole concern has not been found. That is a desirable ditch, as there never was a drop of blood in it, and it is *the* place of all others where there is no dying. Thousands of legs stride over it at "Fishing Creek" and "Fort Donelson" rates, but they never stop to kick the bucket there. But if you want to see fighting, let a company of these *braves* be sent out to defend themselves against some Union Thermopylae where the Spartans are unarmed, and you will see the Southern-Rights men "die in the last ditch."

Wednesday, Feb. 19—Two additional regiments arrived from the South. Town overrun with troops, cutting up all sorts of shines, and taking possession of all vacant houses, and of the Methodist white and colored houses of worship in East Knoxville.

Captain Latrobe, a Baltimorean, of the artillery service, ordered to guard my house until otherwise instructed. The captain has acted the gentleman towards us, and his men are behaving very well.

Thursday, Feb. 20—The remains of Captain Hugh L. McClung, Jr., who was killed at Fort Donelson, were interred to-day with military honors. I knew him well. He was very clever, and as a *merchant* and *man* I liked him. The insane madness of his relatives in favor of this rebellion had much to do with causing him to rush into this war. They would now reflect upon themselves, but that they have all learned the Southern slang of the righteousness of the Rebel cause and the sacredness of the Southern soil. Well, every man to his notion!

Captain Monsarrat returned to-day from Nashville, and is again in command of this post, Colonel Vance having gone to Cumberland Gap with his regiment.

Friday, Feb. 21—Two regiments from Georgia and Mississippi left for the Gap to-day. Their departure has given relief to the citizens. Whilst here, they have denounced, in unmeasured terms, Sneed, Crozier, McAdoo, Charlton, and Graves, and other Southern-Rights champions, for their inglorious flight. The Cleveland (Tenn.) *Banner* is also down upon them for fleeing in such hot haste.

Saturday, Feb. 22—Governor Harris, since his precipitate flight to Memphis, has issued a call for the entire militia of the State to be mustered into service. He even proposes to take the field himself, provided, in his alarm, he can halt long enough to organize.

Sunday, Feb. 23—The two Methodist houses of worship in East Knoxville are to-day occupied with swearing and card-playing troops, and the congregations are driven out. The churches in the old part of the city are not disturbed, because their *pious* pastors are Secessionists, as well as their congregations, to some extent, while those in East Knoxville are for the Union, first, last, and all the time.

Monday, Feb. 24—I have this day sent to Captain Monsarrat, commanding this post, to consult him about letting me out of the Confederacy. He informs me that he has just received a dispatch from General [John H.] Winder, commanding at Richmond, ordering him to deliver me to him in that city. I don't like this indication: it looks to me like another intended violation of faith, and as though I am to be badly treated.

Tuesday, Feb. 25—The town and county are both said to be in a perfect uproar, on account of the Governor's call for the militia. All hands are out, offering to raise companies, so as to avoid being drafted—all wanting to be *captains*, none prepared to enter the service as *privates*.

Wednesday, Feb. 26—A company of blackguards and vagabonds, called cavalry, rode by my house to-day, some of whom cursed and denounced my wife, who sat at the window sewing. These are some of the cowardly devils who ran from "Fishing Creek," and have been fitted out with new horses. A company of them can demolish any unarmed Union *woman* in the country!

Thursday, Feb. 27—I addressed the following card to Secretary Benjamin to-day:

Knoxville, Feb. 27, 1862

Hon. J. P. Benjamin:

Satisfied, upon reliable information, that my personal safety forbids my going out of this Confederacy by way of Richmond, I ask the justice to allow Major Monsarrat to send me through the lines, either over Cumberland Mountain or *via* Nashville. I prefer the latter, as I am not yet well enough to undergo the fatigues of travelling on horseback.

Very respectfully, &c.,

W. G. Brownlow

Friday, Feb. 28—This is Jeff Davis's day for fasting, humiliation, and prayer; and if ever a set of men needed to humble themselves before God and confess their sins, it is the men associated with him in this infernal rebellion. The hypocrites of the town, and many false pretenders to extraordinary piety, will, no doubt, turn out *in force*. The day is beautiful, the sky clear and serene, without a cloud; and the Rebels will, no doubt, flatter themselves that Providence is favoring them with good weather. This is a mistake: Providence is only drying up the roads [so] that the Federal army can get at the retreating forces of the demoralized army of the South.

Saturday, March 1—The elections came off to-day for sheriffs and other county officers, and, as far as returns have come in, the Union ticket prevails. Ay, and it always will prevail in East Tennessee, unless the present race of voters are extinguished.

Thirty Union men, well dressed, were arrested by the cavalry, who found them leaving for Kentucky, to avoid the draft ordered by Governor Harris. Seventeen of them agreed to join the Confederate army, to keep out of jail.

But a Sabbath past, they brought twenty Union men out of jail, arms tied behind them with strong ropes, and marched them with bayonets

to the depot, cursing and insulting them, and sent them off to Tuscaloosa, to be held as prisoners during the war. To have seen them coming out of the jail-yard and entering the street, would have brought
tears from the eyes of the unfeeling Sepoys of India.

Sunday, March 2—The following dispatch has just been received by
Major Monsarrat, the officer in command of this post, and read to me
by that officer:

Richmond, March 2, 1862

MAJOR MONSARRAT:
  You are authorized to send Brownlow out of Tennessee by the Cumberland
Mountains, or any other safe road.

J. P. BENJAMIN,
Secretary of War

As clouds of darkness are gathering around me, and dangers are
multiplying in every direction, I have resolved, feeble as I am, to go,
and I have notified the officer that I shall be ready to leave by morning,
selecting as my route the railroad to Nashville. I will continue my
journal on the road, if I can do so without detection.

Monday night, March 3—I left home this morning at seven o'clock,
with an escort of four citizens, under command of Adjutant-General
[H. C.] Young and Lieutenant [John W.] O'Brien, officers of my own
selection; and upon reaching Loudon, thirty miles west of Knoxville,
we were furnished with ten armed soldiers for an escort. These men
were taken from Captain Dill's company of East Tennessee troops. Before starting, the captain made substantially this speech to his men:

  Soldiers! you are to escort Parson Brownlow to Nashville, under the command of these officers. He is sent out by the Confederate Government; and
your duty is to protect him from insult and injury, at all hazards, come from
what source they may. Treat him courteously and kindly, and discharge your
duty as men, though you are engaged in a cause he opposes.

  I feel grateful to Captain Dill for this manly advice to his men, and
I have so far found his men of the right grit.
  At Athens, some sixty miles west of Knoxville, we met a train filled

with drunken vagabonds, on furlough, returning towards Yorktown [Virginia]. They learned that I was on board, and made a rush towards my car, but were repulsed by my guard, placed on the rear and front platforms by officer Young. This day has brought us to Bridgeport [Alabama], on the Tennessee River, where we are all to lie over until to-morrow morning, when the Nashville train passes. . . .

Wartrace Depot [Tennessee], Friday, March 7—We arrived here three days ago, and have all been detained for the want of authority from one of the Confederate generals to raise a flag of truce and proceed within the Federal lines. Moreover, the rolling stock on the [rail]road to Murfreesborough, leading to Nashville, has all been withdrawn. We have sent Mr. [Samuel H.] Rogers, a civilian, but one of our escort, to Shelbyville, on a branch [rail]road, only eight miles distant, to ask of General [William J.] Hardee, in command of some ten or fifteen thousand troops at that post, to grant us a flag of truce. Rogers is back, and reports that Hardee refuses the flag. We have started Lieutenant O'Brien and Rogers to Huntsville, to head the Confederate generals [Albert Sidney] Johnston, [George] Crittenden, [William H.] Carroll, [Thomas C.] Hindman, [John C.] Breckinridge, [John] Floyd, and [Gideon] Pillow, in their precipitate flight into North Alabama. Our messengers came up with General Albert Sidney Johnston at Huntsville, and obtained the following remarkable document:

> Head-Quarters, Confederate District,
> Huntsville, March 7, 1862
>
> LIEUTENANT O'BRIEN, *Third Tennessee Regiment*:
> SIR: General A. S. Johnston, having just heard that you have brought W. G. Brownlow to Wartrace, as a prisoner, instructs you to return him to his home, or release him where he now is, as he may elect.
> Respectfully,
>
> W. W. MACKALL

This order to return me to my home was in effect to send me back into the lions' den; and the one to turn me loose at Wartrace was to hand me over to [John Hunt] Morgan's mob of cavalry, who were eager to get hold of me. Lieutenant O'Brien telegraphed us that Johnston had given this order, and we telegraphed back for him to follow on to Decatur [Alabama] and demand of General Crittenden a flag of truce, exhibiting to him our passports from the War Department. I hope before a great while that the Federal army may capture this man *A. Sidney Johnston*, and not release him until the war is over.

Lieutenant O'Brien came up with General Crittenden at Decatur, and obtained from him the following very different order:

> Head-Quarters, Second Division,
> Central Army, March 8, 1862

In obedience to the orders of the Secretary of War of the Confederate States, the officers in charge of W. G. Brownlow will conduct him, under a flag of truce, to the most convenient and practicable point of the lines of the enemy, and deliver him over to the Federal authorities.

By command of Major-General Crittenden.

> POLLOCK B. LEE,
> *Assist. Adjt.-General*

With this authority we came on to Shelbyville, and, to our astonishment, found this document, and the order of the War Department at Richmond, wholly insufficient to pass us through the Rebel lines, where Brigadier-General Hardee was in command, as the sequel will show. At the dirty hotel at Wartrace, where we could get nothing fit to eat, and had to lodge in a filthy room on still more filthy Secession beds, we paid, for six of us, for three days, SIXTY DOLLARS!

Shelbyville, March 14—We have now been here seven days, being refused, by *General Hardee*, the privilege of proceeding to Nashville. Major [W. D.] Pickett, a member of General Hardee's staff, called upon one of the officers having me in charge, and signified the general's intention to dispatch me to Montgomery, Alabama, and confine me in jail. He was told that, with the documents I held from the War Department and from General Crittenden, it would be a disgrace to the Confederate Government to re-arrest and imprison me.

There were some drunken scoundrels here from East Tennessee, connected with the army, who, upon our arrival, infused into the already corrupt and poisoned mind of this humbug of an officer, Hardee, all the hatred they could, and sought to prevent my safe conduct beyond the Rebel lines. A panic prevailed among these cowardly rascals, equal to that which backed them out from "Fishing Creek," Fort Donelson, and Bowling Green [Kentucky], and they were not inclined to respect the orders of their superior officers.

The truth is, this man Hardee is engaged in removing their Government stores to Georgia, Mississippi, and Alabama; and they are working in dread of [Union] General [Don Carlos] Buell's forces, who are only fifty miles distant. They feared—and so expressed themselves— that if I got through the lines safe I would inform the enemy of their condition and have them all bagged. I greatly prefer their being bagged down on the line of the Cotton States; and I am well enough posted to justify the prediction that this will be done before a great while. May God hasten the hour!

They had on hand, when I first arrived here, the bacon of *twenty-nine thousand hogs*, and the meat of *two thousand beeves*. They have seized upon the negroes and wagons of the citizens indiscriminately, and used them in brisk style to haul to the depot. In these hurried movements they have, nevertheless, discovered that the bacon of some *fourteen hundred hogs* is missing. They have instituted a search, and found the bacon of *two hundred* of their missing hogs in the basement story of a large brick house, one mile from town, occupied by the *father of the contractor with the Rebel Government*! This lot has just been captured by General Hardee and sent off on the trains; but no punishment is to be inflicted upon the thieves, as they are all Secessionists.

This man Hardee has demanded that "this Brownlow demonstration" shall cease; by which he means the visits of Union men to my room, and the visits of Union ladies, who all sympathize with me. This is Bedford county, and Shelbyville is the county town, and both are strongly Union; while the presence of a demoralized Southern army has only had the effect to increase the devotion of the people to the Union. Hardee is by no means adding strength to the Rebel cause. He is the well-known humbug whose book of "Tactics" is in use in the army. The translation is from the French: it was made in Philadelphia, by an officer of the army, and Hardee fathered the production, and claims the authorship of what he had not the ability to produce. This is known to the army-officers North, and has increased their contempt for this foolish and weak man. Hatred to General [Winfield] Scott, by Jeff Davis, while [U.S.] Secretary of War, instigated him to employ his willing tool, Hardee, to get up this new system of "Tactics," which was intended to displace Scott's able work. The lake that burns "with fire and brimstone" will yearn for its promised aliment, until such men as these get there. The time is, however, rapidly approaching when the wailings of their damned ghosts will rise upon the flames, and, with one loud, deep, long wail, in bitter utterances of remorse, they will exclaim, "This Rebellion is a failure!"

I have never been more kindly treated than since I came here— ladies and gentlemen visiting me every day, and expressing their kind regards for me. As a specimen, I give the following correspondence between the lady-like daughter of the mayor and myself.

Shelbyville, Tennessee, March 11, 1862

Rev. W. G. Brownlow:

Dear Sir: Herewith I send you a collection of flowers, which I beg you will do me the favor to accept as a small token of the high esteem which I cherish for you on account of your great devotion to, and untiring efforts in behalf of, our once-glorious Union; and beg to express the hope that the Government established by our fathers will yet be sustained, and bound together by stronger ties than those by which we have heretofore been united.

With sentiments of highest esteem,

I beg to remain your friend,

Edith J. Galbraith

Shelbyville, Tenn., March 13, 1862

Miss Edith J. Galbraith:

During the six days I have been detained here I have been called upon by a number of the ladies of Shelbyville, both married and single, who have, in words of kindness, expressed their sympathies for me in my departure from by home and family. These evidences of regard have greatly comforted me, after my confinement in a crowded and uncomfortable *jail* for having reiterated to the people of East Tennessee what Washington taught us—namely, that "The Constitution is sacredly obligatory upon all"; and for having proclaimed, as Jackson did, "The Union—it must be preserved."

But your kind note of the 11th instant, and the accompanying "collection of flowers," have afforded me a pleasure for which I have no words suitably to express my thanks. I shall at least carry these flowers with me to the redeemed and disenthralled capital of our State, where I can see the glorious Stars and Stripes of our distracted country floating from the dome of the capitol.

I hope at no distant day to visit your noble Union town again, when, I feel perfectly confident, our loyal State—rushed out of the Union, at the point of the bayonet, under the lead of her worst men—will be back in the old Union, and her citizens, contented and happy, determined never again to embark in the hell-born and hell-bound cause of Secession.

I am, very respectfully, &c.,

W. G. Brownlow

I will record an incident that occurred on the train as I came to this point and to Wartrace, some ten days ago, and then close out my sojourn in Shelbyville. A tall, self-important Rebel officer, dressed in a full suit of uniform, learning at the depot that I was on board, came into the car, and inquired of one of our guards if I was on board, and, being told that I was, said, "Show me Brownlow." The guard pointed out Adjutant-General Young—a very fine-looking man, dressed in citizen's clothes—and said, "That is Brownlow, with the slouch-cap on." He gazed at him. He frowned with the scowl of a demon, wrinkled his brow, and, with a sour, sullen, frowning look, exclaimed, "I am satisfied. He is a mean-looking man. I believe all I have heard about him." Thus he retired, passing sentence against a clever gentleman and a man of really fine personal appearance. This shows what prejudice will do. Here was an officer in the Confederate ranks condemned as worthy of death for a *supposed bad countenance*, because he was erroneously reported to be a man against whom all Rebeldom entertains a strong prejudice.

Nashville, March 15—To-day, at twelve o'clock, I was landed within the Federal lines, having come from Shelbyville, at a rapid rate, on the Nolensville turnpike. We had up the white flag when we came upon the pickets. They halted us, and inquired by what authority we had that flag of truce up. I alighted from the buggy, and introduced myself to them as "Parson Brownlow"—when, with one accord, they advanced and gave me a cordial shake of the hand. They said they had heard of me before, and were glad that I had come within their lines.

I was sent for by Colonel [James S.] Jackson, an ex-Congressman, and a noble Kentucky gentleman, commanding a regiment of cavalry. I was treated with great kindness and with marked attention by the officers, while the privates crowded around to see me upon the mention of my name. I *felt* and *knew* that I was among friends. Nay, I felt like a bird out of a cage. Brigadier-General [Thomas J.] Wood, a noble son of Kentucky, within whose division we were (five miles distant from Nashville), came up to receive our flag of truce; and a more cordial welcome no man ever received. He at once commissioned Captain Leonard, of his staff, to turn me over to General Buell, the chief in command. Our only trouble was in regard to Lieutenant O'Brien, a Rebel officer, who, if admitted into Nashville, must be blind-folded. However, General Buell met me with the same cordiality with which I had been greeted before, and said that my friends—O'Brien, Rogers, Harrison, and others—should lodge with me at the hotel: accordingly, we were all landed at the St. Cloud Hotel.

General Buell, as I understand, is a native of Indiana, or hails from there. He is a man of liberal education and cultivated tastes—a man of fine conversational powers, and a chivalrous, high-toned gentleman. Below six feet, he is heavily built, with an eagle eye. He was dressed in a handsome uniform, with a sort of foraging-cap. He has a fair complexion and blonde moustache, with suavity and politeness written in every line of his face. I take him to be about forty-five years of age—certainly not so much as fifty. He has *ninety thousand men* here, and more arriving every day. He has the confidence of his command, and will move his forces in a few days into Alabama. He asked me many questions, in quick succession, touching East Tennessee. I answered him promptly, and, as I have reason to believe, quite to his satisfaction.

Nashville, March 20—I have here found Governor [Andrew] Johnson, Horace Maynard, Emerson Etheridge,[11] and Colonel Trigg—all in good health, and glad to see me landed safe in the *United States*. Governor Johnson is here as Military Governor, with the rank of brigadier-general, and is now organizing a State Government. . . .

11. Maynard, a U.S. congressman from East Tennessee, and Etheridge, a former U.S. congressman from West Tennessee, were two of the most prominent Unionist leaders in the state.

The Secessionists regard the appointment of Governor Johnson as a very unfortunate one; but the Union men, irrespective of old party associations, regard it as most fortunate, and say that we have the right man in the right place. I have no doubt his appointment to the office will give general satisfaction to Union men throughout the State. I am certain this will be the case in East Tennessee.

The feeling of opposition to the Federal Government and the occupation of this city by Federal troops is gradually giving way to a spirit of acquiescence, and to the "sober second thought" of sensible and patriotic men. The good order, strict discipline, and sober habits of *one hundred thousand troops* here are in striking contrast with the thieving, drinking, and other revolting habits of the so-called Confederate soldiers, who but recently committed all manner of outrages in these streets. Even the children and negroes see and speak of the difference.

The ladies of Nashville are more bitter and unyielding in their hostility to the Federal army than any other class of citizens. I can excuse them: most of them have sons, brothers, or husbands in the Rebel army, and they regard Federal officers and soldiers as their enemies, in search of their relatives. . . .

My room was entered last evening by some officers and civilians from Kentucky, and I was literally forced out into the crowd, in front of the St. Cloud Hotel, where a speech was demanded. I sought to be excused; but they would take no denial, and I proceeded to deliver this speech:

SPEECH OF W. G. BROWNLOW IN NASHVILLE

GENTLEMEN: I am in a sad plight to say much of interest—too thoroughly incapacitated to do justice to you or myself. My throat has been disordered for the past three years, and I have been compelled to almost abandon public speaking. Last December I was thrust into an uncomfortable and disagreeable jail—for what? *Treason!* Treason to the bogus Confederacy; and the proofs of that treason were articles which appeared in the *Knoxville Whig* in May last, when the State of Tennessee was a member of the imperishable Union. At the expiration of four weeks I became a victim of the typhoid fever, and was removed to a room in a decent dwelling, and a guard of seven men kept me company. I subsequently became so weak that I could not turn over in my bed, and the guard was increased to twelve men, for fear I should suddenly recover and run away to Kentucky. But I never had any intention to run, and, if I had, I was not able to escape. My purpose was to make them send me out of their infamous Government, according to contract, or to hang me, if they thought proper. I was promised passports by their Secretary of War, a little Jew, late of New Orleans; and upon the faith of that promise, and upon the invitation of General Crittenden, then in command at Knoxville, I reported myself and demanded my passports. They gave me passports, but they were from my house to the Knoxville jail, and the escort was a deputy marshal of Jeff Davis. But I served my time out, and have been landed here at last, through much tribulation. When I started on this perilous journey, I was sore distressed both in mind and body, being weak from disease and confinement. I expected to meet with insults and indignities at every point from the black-guard portion of the Rebel soldiers and citizens, and in this I was not disap-pointed. It was fortunate, indeed, that I was not mobbed. This would have been done, but for the vigilance and fidelity of the officers having me in com-mand. These were Adjutant-General Young and Lieutenant O'Brien, clever men, high-minded, and honorable; and they were of my own selection. They had so long been Union men that I felt assured they had not lost the instincts of gentlemen and patriots, afflicted as they were with the incurable disease of Secession!

But, gentlemen, some three or four days ago I landed in this city, as you are aware. Five miles distant I encountered the Federal pickets. Then it was that I felt like a new man. My depression ceased, and returning life and health seemed suddenly to invigorate my system and to arouse my physical constitu-tion. I had been looking at soldiers in uniform for twelve months, and to me they appeared as hateful as their Confederacy and their infamous flag. But these Federal pickets, who received me kindly and shook me cordially by the hand, looked like angels of light, compared with the insulting blackguards who had been groaning and cursing around my house.

Why, my friends, these demagogues actually boast that the Lord is upon their side, and declare that God Almighty is assisting them in the furtherance of their nefarious project. In Knoxville and surrounding localities, a short time since, daily prayer-meetings were held, wherein the Almighty was be-seeched to raise Lincoln's blockade and to hurl destruction against the Burn-side Expedition. Their prayers were partly answered: the blockade at Roa-noke Island was most effectually raised!

Gentlemen, I am no Abolitionist; I applaud no sectional doctrines. I am a Southern man, and all my relatives and interests are thoroughly identified with the South and Southern institutions. I was born in the Old Dominion; my parents were born in Virginia, and they and their ancestors were all slaveholders. Let me assure you that the South has suffered no infringement upon her institutions; the Slavery question was actually *no* pretext for this unholy, unrighteous conflict. Twelve Senators from the Cotton States, who had sworn to preserve inviolate the Constitution framed by our forefathers, plotted treason at night—a fit time for such a crime—and telegraphed to their States dispatches advising them to pass ordinances of secession. Yes, gentlemen, twelve Senators swore allegiance in the day-time, and unswore it at night.

Soldiers and citizens! Secession is well-nigh played out—the dog is dead—and their demoralized army are on their way to the Cotton States where they can look back at you, as you approach their scattered lines.[12] I have been detained among them for ten days, General Hardee refusing to let me pass. This was only fifty-five miles from here, in the sound Union town of Shelbyville. They were pushing off their bacon and flour and their demoralized men; and I hope you will follow them up. You will overtake them at the Tennessee River—sooner, if they come up with new supplies of mean whiskey.

But, gentlemen, you see that I am growing hoarse in this fierce wind. I am otherwise feeble, not having attempted to make a speech in months. Excuse me, therefore, and join me in this sentiment, should this wicked and unholy war continue—"Grape for the Rebel masses, and hemp for their leaders!" . . .[13]

Crosswicks, N. J., May 10 [1862]—I am now in a pleasant and quiet village in New Jersey, county of Burlington—a county wanting but a few hundred inhabitants to equal in population the entire State of Florida. Here I have reposed in quiet and comfort, for three weeks, in the hospitable mansion of Robert E. Peterson, Esq., whose extensive library has been at my command whilst I have hurried through with this book. . . .

My wife and children have arrived in New Jersey, after a long and

12. Brownlow's optimistic belief that the Confederacy was on its last legs—thanks to the recent stunning successes of the Union Army in Tennessee—was shared by many northerners and southern Unionists at this time. A series of Union military setbacks loomed ahead, however, and the Confederacy would survive for three more years.

13. Brownlow left Nashville around March 22 and headed north to begin his speaking tour. A few weeks later he settled in New Jersey to write his book.

fatiguing journey, *via* Fortress Monroe [Virginia], under a flag of truce, and after the sacrifice of a large and well-furnished house and all I have succeeded in accumulating during twenty-five years of toil and industry. . . ..

The work of murder, arrests, and imprisonments goes bravely on in East Tennessee, as my family inform me, who left Knoxville six weeks after I did.[14] They were shooting Union men down in the streets, arresting hundreds, and killed, in one instance, fifty or sixty after they had surrendered and were under an arrest. They marched between three and four hundred loyal citizens, some of them barefooted and their feet bleeding, to the depot, and shipped them to Atlanta, Georgia, to work upon their fortifications. These men were denied water: they would lift out of *mud-puddles* in the streets, with their hands, after a rain, what they could to quench their thirst.

In God's name, I call upon President Lincoln, and upon his Cabinet and army-officers, to say how long they will suffer a loyal people, true to the Union and to the Government of their fathers, to suffer in this way. The Union men of East Tennessee are largely in the majority—say three to one—but they have no arms; they are in the jails of the country; they are working on Rebel fortifications, like slaves under the lash, and no Federal force has ever yet been marched into that oppressed and down-trodden country. Let the Government, if it have any regard for its obligations, redeem that country at once, and liberate these people, no matter at what cost of blood and treasure. They have suffered these outrages for the last twelve months, and are now desponding—nay, despairing of any relief.

Let an army—"a terrible army, with banners"—go at once into East Tennessee, and back up the loyal citizens, while the latter shoot and hang their persecutors wherever they can find them. I want the army to serve for me as a forerunner—a sort of John the Baptist in the wilderness—so that I may go back with a new press, type, and paper, and resurrect my Union journal, and tell one hundred thousand subscribers, weekly, what is going on upon the borders of civilization. . . .

14. This paragraph and the two following are a letter to the editor of a Philadelphia newspaper that Brownlow wrote while in New Jersey; he reproduced the entire letter in his book.

I have now finished this sketch of Secession by an eye-witness. It has been a sad record. I have no particle of sympathy for the leaders in this criminal rebellion; but I commiserate the multitudes who have been swept into its vortex by a current of overwhelming fanaticism and terrorism which they were powerless to resist. I have spoken plainly, vehemently—perhaps bitterly: I could not do otherwise in so dear a concernment as my country's good. I feel that I may appropriate the prophet's language: the "word was in mine heart as a burning fire shut up in my bones; I was weary with forbearing, and could not stay." I can spare no denunciation when I see demagogues and traitors deliberately plunging us into a fratricidal war fit only for the leadership of Cain. But I lay down my pen with the conviction that the bold, bad men who have appealed to the arbitrament of arms will be discomfited in that issue. The thronging victories of the Constitution are the presages of returning peace and prosperity. God grant that the people may now raise their eyes and lift their hands to the eternal and propitious Throne, in fervent supplication that the Father of Mercies will compose the distractions of our suffering land, and eclipse the splendor of our annals in the past by the future renown, for ages to come, of the Re-United States!

THE END

SELECTED BIBLIOGRAPHY

✝

Alexander, Thomas B. "Introduction." In William G. Brownlow, *Sketches of the Rise, Progress, and Decline of Secession; with a Narrative of Personal Adventures among the Rebels*, v–xix. Philadelphia, 1862. Reprint. New York, 1968.

———. *Political Reconstruction in Tennessee*. Nashville, 1950. Reprint. New York, 1968.

———. "Strange Bedfellows: The Interlocking Careers of T. A. R. Nelson, Andrew Johnson, and W. G. (Parson) Brownlow." East Tennessee Historical Society's *Publications* 24(1952):68–91.

Atkins, Jonathan M. *Parties, Politics, and the Sectional Conflict in Tennessee, 1832–1861*. Knoxville, 1997.

Bergeron, Paul H. *Antebellum Politics in Tennessee*. Lexington, 1982.

Conklin, Forrest. "Parson Brownlow Joins the Sons of Temperance." *Tennessee Historical Quarterly* 39(1980):178–94, 292–309.

———, and John W. Wittig. "Religious Warfare in the Southern Highlands: Brownlow versus Ross." *Journal of East Tennessee History* 63(1991):33–50.

Coulter, E. Merton. *William G. Brownlow, Fighting Parson of the Southern Highlands*. Chapel Hill, 1937. Reprint. Knoxville, 1971, 1999.

Crofts, Daniel W. *Reluctant Confederates: Upper South Unionists in the Secession Crisis*. Chapel Hill, 1989.

Fisher, Noel C. "Definitions of Loyalty: Unionist Histories of the Civil War in East Tennessee." *Journal of East Tennessee History* 67(1995):58–88.

———. *War at Every Door: Partisan Politics and Guerrilla Violence in East Tennessee, 1860–1869*. Chapel Hill, 1997.

Haskins, Ralph W. "Internecine Strife in Tennessee: Andrew Johnson versus Parson Brownlow." *Tennessee Historical Quarterly* 24(1965):321–40.

Humes, Thomas William. *The Loyal Mountaineers of Tennessee*. Knoxville, 1888. Reprint. Spartanburg, 1974.

Humphrey, Steve. *"That D——d Brownlow": Being a Saucy and Malicious Description of William Gannaway Brownlow.* . . . Boone, 1978.

Kelly, James C. "William Gannaway Brownlow." *Tennessee Historical Quarterly* 43(1984):25–43, 155–72.

Lattimore, R. B. "A Survey of William G. Brownlow's Criticisms of the Mormons, 1841–1857." *Tennessee Historical Quarterly* 27(1968):249–56.

Noe, Kenneth W., and Shannon H. Wilson, eds. *The Civil War in Appalachia: Collected Essays*. Knoxville, 1997.

Patton, James Welch. "The Senatorial Career of William G. Brownlow." *Tennessee Historical Magazine* 1(1930–31):153–64.

———. *Unionism and Reconstruction in Tennessee, 1860–1869*. Chapel Hill, 1934. Reprint. Gloucester, 1966.

Queener, Verton M. "William G. Brownlow as an Editor." East Tennessee Historical Society's *Publications* 4(1932):67–82.

Temple, Oliver Perry. *East Tennessee and the Civil War*. Cincinnati, 1899. Reprint. Knoxville, 1972.

———. *Notable Men of Tennessee from 1833 to 1875: Their Times and Their Contemporaries*. New York, 1912.

INDEX

†

Abolitionists: criticized by Brownlow, 4, 23, 26, 34, 64; mentioned, 33, 33n, 34, 58, 63, 68
Aristocrats, 32, 40

Baxter, John, 102, 123, 123n, 134
Bell, John, 27, 27n, 31, 50
Benjamin, Judah P., 101–102, 116, 126, 128, 138, 139, 147
Blount, William, 83, 83n
Breckinridge, John C., 27, 27n, 31, 50
Bridge-burning, 94, 94n, 96, 97–98, 111, 113, 117
Brownlow, William G.
—experiences and activities: prewar life and career of, 1, 2–5, 15–19, 36; publishes newspaper, 1, 2, 5, 7, 18, 39–40, 41, 42, 54; tours North, 1, 5, 7, 14, 148n; prepares book, 1, 4, 5–6, 7, 26n, 46n, 47n, 60n, 68n, 71n, 148–49, 148n; indictment and arrest of, 5, 74–76, 102–106, 108–10, 126; imprisonment of, 5, 89, 106–29 passim; refuses Confederate oath, 5, 8, 75, 76–77, 115; writes gallows speech, 5, 125–29; banishment of, to North, 5, 115, 116, 129–30, 138, 139; and escort to Nashville, 5, 139–44; in Nashville, 5, 7, 144–48; as candidate and officeholder, 7–8, 19, 19n, 40, 42, 44–55; post-1862 career of, 7–8; criticism and harassment of, by secessionists, 35–36, 39–40, 63, 65, 67, 73–74; flies U.S. flag, 61–63; harassment of, by soldiers, 61, 73–74, 91–93, 93–94, 96; treasonous editorials of, 71–73, 75, 104–105, 105–106, 106, 108–10, 126; farewell editorial of, 74–78; denies treason charge, 75–76, 99; and newspaper shutdown, 74, 76, 78n, 93, 98–99; flees to mountains, 94–95; negotiates surrender to authorities, 95–102, 126; denies bridge-burning, 96, 97–98; aids condemned man's daughter, 120–22; and Unionist women, 120, 142, 143–44; confinement of, to

Washington, George, 11, 19, 57, 61, 143
Webb, James Watson, 63, 63*n*
Webster, Daniel, 19
Whig. See Knoxville *Whig*
Whigs, 2, 19
Women, 120, 120–22, 123–25, 130, 133, 142, 143, 146, 149

Wood, W. B., 93–94, 94–95, 96, 126

Yancey, William L., 33, 33*n*, 57, 127
Yeomen, 31–32, 44

Zollicoffer, Felix K., 84, 93, 96, 106, 119, 135

CPSIA information can be obtained
at www.ICGtesting.com
Printed in the USA
LVHW080941240123
737820LV00003B/89

9 780807 123546